WITHDRAWN

Magic Search

Getting the Best Results from Your Catalog and Beyond

Rebecca S. Kornegay, Heidi E. Buchanan,
and Hildegard B. Morgan

American Library Association
Chicago   2009

Rebecca S. Kornegay is head of reference at Western Carolina University's Hunter Library in Cullowhee, North Carolina. She received her MSLS from the University of North Carolina at Chapel Hill in 1977. **Heidi E. Buchanan** is a reference librarian at Hunter Library. Her MSLS is from the University of North Carolina at Chapel Hill (2000). **Hildegard B. Morgan** is assistant head of cataloging at Hunter Library. Morgan has thirty years of cataloging experience and also serves at Hunter's reference desk. Kornegay, Buchanan, and Morgan are the coauthors of "Amazing Magic Searches! Subdivisions Combine the Precision of the Cataloger with the Freewheeling Style of a Googler," published in *Library Journal*, November 2005.

The paper used in this publication meets the minimum requirements of American National Standard for Information Sciences—Permanence of Paper for Printed Library Materials, ANSI Z39.48-1992. ∞

Library of Congress Cataloging-in-Publication Data
Kornegay, Rebecca S.
    Magic search : getting the best results from your catalog and beyond / Rebecca S. Kornegay, Heidi E. Buchanan, and Hildegard B. Morgan.
        p. cm.
    Includes bibliographical references and index.
    ISBN 978-0-8389-0990-4 (alk. paper)
    1. Subject heading subdivisions—Handbooks, manuals, etc. 2. Subject headings, Library of Congress—Handbooks, manuals, etc. 3. Online library catalogs—Subject access—Handbooks, manuals, etc. I. Buchanan, Heidi E. II. Morgan, Hildegard B. III. Title.

Z695.Z8L52375 2009
025.4'7—dc22   2008052519

ISBN-13: 978-0-8389-0990-4

Printed in the United States of America
13   12   11   10   09   5   4   3   2   1

CONTENTS

Introduction   v

Using the Book   xi

1. Finding Basic Treatments and Background Reading   1

2. Finding How-To Guides   4

3. Finding Images   9

4. Words, Words, . . . and Numbers   14

5. Finding Out about People: Individuals and Groups   22

6. Finding Out about Places   36

7. Finding Creative Treatments: Stories, Poems, Songs, etc.   40

8. Finding True Stories: Memoirs, Observations, and Confessions   43

9. Finding Primary Sources   45

10. It's about Time: Time Periods and Chronological Subdivisions   48

11. Tools for Scholars and Other Professionals   52

12. Subdivisions That Give Perspective, Put You in Control, and Amaze Others!   55

13. Useful for the Humanities   59

14. Useful for the Social Sciences   73

15. Useful for Historical Research   82

16. Useful for Business Topics   89

17. Useful for Education Topics   95

18. Useful for Natural and Physical Sciences   98

19. **Useful for Medicine and Health Topics**   **109**

20. **Useful for Technology Topics**   **115**

21. **The Baby and the Bathwater: Recommendations**   **118**

Acknowledgments   123
Works Cited   125
Index   127

INTRODUCTION

DEFINITION OF A SUBDIVISION

This book is all about Library of Congress subdivisions; so, let's start with a definition from Lois Chan (2005, 91): "In the Library of Congress subject headings system, a main heading may be subdivided by one or more elements called *subdivisions*. . . . Subdivisions are used extensively to subarrange a large file or to bring out aspects of a topic." The first segment of a subject heading, called the main heading, tells what the book is about. The subdivisions follow the main heading, introduced by a dash, and add specificity. They tell which aspect of the main topic is treated; describe the format of the cataloged item; and, in some cases, state the geographic area or chronological time period covered.

Here's an example: In the subject heading **Roofing--Amateurs' manuals**, **Roofing** is the main heading; **--Amateurs' manuals** is the subdivision. In the subject heading **Tobacco--Physiological effect--Charts, diagrams, etc.**, both **--Physiological effect** and **--Charts, diagrams, etc.** are subdivisions.

WHY DEVOTE AN ENTIRE BOOK TO LIBRARY OF CONGRESS SUBDIVISIONS?

The effective use of subdivisions in searching is essential in a time when libraries talk constantly about the need "to optimize resource discovery for their patrons" (ALCTS 2008, para. 1). And as you will see later in this introduction, subdivisions are showing up in new places, like Google Book Search, and as options to refine in faceted searches. With this book, we intend to empower our readers with lists of the very best subdivisions, explained and organized for ready use by librarians who want to produce amazing search results.

The project began in 2005, with an article for *Library Journal* titled "Amazing Magic Searches! Subdivisions Combine the Precision of the Cataloger with the Freewheeling Style of a Googler." In the article we argued that Library of Congress subdivisions, though unassuming in appearance, are in reality the most powerful controlled vocabulary of all. We recommended that reference librarians learn and use subdivisions, and we offered a list of twenty-five top performers. We explained, "Subdivisions perform magic in a library catalog, allowing librarians to finesse their keyword searches in ways that astonish amateurs. They replace the sometimes disparate strings of key-words searchers use to express the nuances of their questions" (Kornegay, Buchanan, and Morgan 2005, 44).

The article was enthusiastically received. Fans included catalogers, ref-erence librarians, and professors, and the article appeared on several blogs, in research guides, and in newsletters. It is being used to train others, and it is included in reading lists for reference and cataloging courses. The most common praise was for the practical usefulness of the list of twenty-five. Buoyed by the positive reception and knowing that there were many more subdivisions that would make a world of difference for searchers, we decided to create a book that would offer ready-to-use lists of the best Library of Con-gress subdivisions.

MAKING THE LIST, CHECKING IT THRICE—AND THEN SOME

We had already discovered, during our initial work on the article, the cata-logers' best-kept secret, the *Subject Cataloging Manual: Subject Headings,* where all 3,500-plus subdivisions are listed and defined. These also appear, albeit in a less robust form, in the front of the first volume of *Library of Con-gress Subject Headings,* starting with the twenty-eighth edition, published in 2005.

Now, with a book in mind, we scanned the complete list and flagged any subdivision that looked promising. We then created fifteen "search-use" categories that we would put the subdivisions into—subdivisions for finding images or how-to books, for finding basic treatments of a topic, and so on. With our first-run list of 339 subdivisions in hand and roughly categorized, it was time to delve into the details in the cataloging documentation.

We read mind-boggling rules and instructions in *Subject Cataloging Manual: Subject Headings,* produced by the Library of Congress Cataloging Distribution Service and "the standard for catalogers in all large libraries in the English-speaking world" (Mann 2005, 25). We double-checked each rule in Cataloger's Desktop, the *Subject Cataloging Manual*'s online equivalent, http://desktop.loc.gov (subscription required). We wrestled with subtleties like the distinction between **--Terminology** and **--Terms and phrases**. We let go preconceived notions ("You mean, **--Biography** isn't used for individual people? **--Atlases** doesn't identify books of maps?"). We tested each subdi-vision in library catalogs of all sizes. We eliminated snoozers (**--Legislative history, --Names**), abandoned the overly esoteric (**--Cataphora, --Herbarium**), and picked favorites (**--Essence, genius, nature; --Notebooks, sketchbooks, etc.;**

--**Miscellanea**). While we worked to whittle the list down, other important and intriguing subdivisions emerged and demanded our attention. --**Friends and associates** led to the dishier --**Mistresses** and --**Paramours**. A twelve-page list of subdivisions just for place-names turned up and could not be ignored.

In the end, almost five hundred subdivisions met our tests. This book presents these top performers in clear language and organized by function, in twenty categories for quick reference for practicing librarians.

HOW SUBDIVISIONS WORK

Detailed rules and specific definitions control the way subdivisions are assigned to a cataloged item. We'll use as an example the most common kind of rule, the "attached to" or "goes with" rule. Such rules tell which kind of main heading a particular subdivision may or may not be attached to. For example, a cataloger may not attach the subdivision --**Social life and customs** to the name of an individual. On the other hand, --**Social life and customs** does go with or may be attached to place-names; --**Schooling** goes only with animals; --**Mood** is attached only to languages.

Those rules and definitions, based on scholarship, careful thought, and years of fine work at the Library of Congress, are the foundation of the high-performance catalogs libraries are so proud of, yet reference librarians are unlikely to have the opportunity to learn them well. Guess what? They don't have to! In this book, we will tell you when rules are important and when you can ignore them. And we will translate the definitions into front-of-the-house tools for searching so well that patrons will exclaim, "How did you find that?"

How can we be so nonchalant about the rules? Because in WorldCat and in most library catalogs, subdivisions perform beautifully in keyword searches, whether the searcher knows the rules or not. Keyword searches pull from all the subject headings assigned to a title. Here's an example of a keyword search that succeeds in spite of the "attached to" rule. **Shakespeare and social life and customs** finds

> **TITLE:** Understanding Shakespeare's England
> **SUBJECT HEADINGS:** Shakespeare, William, 564-1616--Contemporary England
> England--Social life and customs--16th century
> England--Civilization--16th century

The conscientious cataloger, adhering to the rules, did not attach --**Social life and customs** to the main heading Shakespeare, but for the searcher it didn't matter. Shakespeare came from one subject heading; social life and customs from another.

What did matter? That the searcher knew to use --**Social life and customs** in the first place. **Shakespeare and social life and customs** replaced the natural language inquiry "How did people live and behave in Shakespeare's time?" and the search succeeded.

WHAT KNOWLEDGE MUST THE LIBRARIAN BRING TO A SEARCH?

Carefree keyword searching is the goal, but reality does intrude on occasion. Throughout our work on this book, we tried to maintain a freewheeling search style and think like a "Googler." Usually it worked, but not always. So, when should a librarian bring out the tools of a professional searcher? And what does matter?

Precision matters. If the subdivision is singular, you'd better use the singular. If it's plural, use the plural. It's **--Influence**, not *influences,* **--Diaries** not *diary.*

Definitions matter. **Nurses--Attitudes** means how nurses feel about things, not the way people feel about nurses. If the precise definitions didn't matter, subdivisions would be useless, as would this book!

Freewheeling searching means results will vary, so librarians must continue to use all of their professional search techniques. Keyword searches pull from more than just subdivisions, finding words from titles, contents notes, and more, so relevance may suffer. In some cases, educated browsing of subdivisions and their corresponding main headings works better than keyword searching, so we may caution you to browse display lists of subject headings and to choose the appropriate subdivision from the list. Finally, a keyword search on a subdivision that is a common word, like *history,* can lead to too many hits, so we suggest you perform a keyword-in-subject search.

In addition, librarians must know how their catalogs work!

- Does your library catalog allow keyword-in-subject searching? (Look for the advanced search option.)
- In a subject search, can you type in a main heading and then browse the accompanying subdivisions?
- Does a subject search in your catalog search each segment of the subject headings? This means that you can type a subdivision into the subject search box, without specifying a main heading.

SUBDIVISIONS AT WORK

A few years ago some predicted that controlled vocabulary would go the way of the dodo. In fact, libraries are reaffirming the value of the Library of Congress subject heading system; catalogs and databases display controlled vocabulary more prominently than before; WorldCat is now freely available to the public; and a most unlikely player, Google, has bought into the system. These changes make searching with subdivisions relevant in settings old and new, large and small, local and international.

Facet-Based Searching

Library catalogs with faceted search capabilities, now more commonplace than newsworthy, alert the searcher to options that are available for any search at any time. These catalogs, often referred to as discovery tools, recommend that the searcher refocus the initial search by selecting from a list of system-suggested subjects, which include Library of Congress subdivisions. The searcher who knows subdivisions will be in a position to make good choices.

WorldCat

The Online Computer Library Center (OCLC) database WorldCat.org is now available free of charge to everyone. WorldCat has millions and millions of records for 1.2 billion items—books, CDs, DVDs, websites—and most of those records include Library of Congress subject headings, complete with subdivisions. WorldCat searchers who replace the guesswork of natural language with the precision of subdivisions will find what they really want—even in this gargantuan wonder.

Google Book Search

An unexpected and exciting development for using subdivisions came via an OCLC news release. On May 19, 2008, OCLC (2008, para. 2) announced an agreement with Google Inc.: "Under terms of the agreement, OCLC member libraries participating in the Google Book Search program, which makes the full text of more than one million books searchable, may share their WorldCat-derived MARC records with Google to better facilitate discovery of library collections through Google."

What does this mean for the subdivision savvy? Google Book Search users can now rely on library-style subject access to more than a million freely available full-text books—the best of both worlds!

SUBDIVISION AWARDS

Every season should end with the presenting of awards! Here are some standouts that will give you a taste of what's to come. Find out why they were nominated in the upcoming chapters! And the nominees are . . .

Congeniality Award (gets along with lots of subjects!)
   --Case studies
   --Chronology
Surprise Hit Award
   --Design and construction
   --Pamphlets
Left-Field Award
   --In bookplates
   --Bonsai collections
Splitting Hairs Award
   --Testing versus --Intelligence testing versus --Psychological testing
   --Tomb versus --Tombs
Most Improved Award
   --Textbooks
Who Knew? Award
   --Essence, genius, nature
   --Portraits, --Art, and the "Rule of A.D. 1400"
Say It Ain't So, LC, Award
   --Controversial literature
   --Personal narratives
Old Dog, New Tricks Award
   --Early works to 1800
Executive Privileges Award
   --Mistresses
   --Paramours

USING THE BOOK

The heart of this book highlights subdivisions according to what they do best. The first eleven chapters present subdivisions that find special formats (e.g., images), special treatments of topics (e.g., fictional, how-to), or certain kinds of information that cross disciplines (information about people and places). We follow with the finesse chapter, "Subdivisions That Give Perspective, Put You in Control, and Amaze Others!" which builds on what readers learned in the previous chapters. The final cluster of chapters lists subdivisions that are useful for different disciplines.

THE ENTRY PARTS

- The subdivision (in boldface)
- Definition or description
- Sample recommended searches (in boldface) and titles that clarify the use of the subdivision.
- Magic Searches, which combine subdivisions to create superpowered search strings
- Rules from the Library of Congress (included only when not knowing the rule would lead the search astray)
- Bonus Features that describe unexpected—and positive—results
- Recommendations to the Library of Congress

OTHER DETAILS

- We use an asterisk (*) as the symbol for truncation.
- Some subdivisions appear in more than one list, because in each different setting a distinct application is featured.

- *See* and *see also* refer to entries elsewhere in this book. *Consider also* refers to subdivisions that we do not cover specifically elsewhere in the book.

CHAPTER 1

Q

FINDING BASIC TREATMENTS
AND BACKGROUND READING

Readers new to a topic often want a basic treatment rather than a treatise written for the expert, yet the Library of Congress offers no single subdivision that leads to overviews or introductions. In fact, most of the books that provide basic treatment of a topic are given just a subject heading—genetics, for example, or philosophy—thus putting them in the vast ocean of general works.

Librarians everywhere use the unflattering workaround "[topic] and dummies," or "[topic] and idiots" to get good results, but surely the Library of Congress could prevent us from stooping to such lowly tactics, so let's start with this:

RECOMMENDATION: The Library of Congress should provide a subdivision for books that treat a subject in a simple and straightforward manner.

Until the Library of Congress comes around, use these seven subdivisions that help identify books that tell who, what, when, and where.

--Outlines, syllabi, etc.
Old-fashioned-sounding but a modern performer, this subdivision finds books that offer "brief statements of the principal elements of a subject to be studied" (Library of Congress 2008a, H1095). **--Outlines, syllabi, etc.** usually offers a structured approach to the subject, breaking the topic down into broad headings and then into subheadings. Combined with topics such as law, philosophy, economics, the immune system, or mysticism, it will deliver a nice selection.

--Textbooks
Introduces us to all kinds of subjects presented "in an organized and simplified manner" (Library of Congress 2008a, H2187). Textbooks are written on every subject imaginable. Whether we thirst for an introduction to audiology, Hindi, the nervous system, heat, electric circuits, psychology, music, or geology, we are sure to find it with **--Textbooks**.

(!) NOTE: Prior to 2002, the Library of Congress limited the use of **--Textbooks** to religious topics and foreign languages (Library of Congress 2008a, H2187).

--Popular works
Top notch! The material presented must address the nonspecialist—most of us, in other words. But beware that **--Popular works** can be attached only to topics in the sciences, in legal disciplines, in technical fields, and in medicine. Does this mean that in all other areas the Library of Congress believes us to be in the know? Should we publicly confess that we lack expertise in quite a few other areas too?

(⊘) RECOMMENDATION: The Library of Congress should extend this subdivision to a broader range of topics. After all, in 2002 **--Textbooks** was finally liberated!

In the meantime, remember, "German language and popular works and grammar," probably by many considered a rather oxymoronic constellation anyway, will not get you anywhere!

--Problems, exercises, etc.
At first glance, this might be dismissed as dealing mainly with mathematical problems. The extra help provided by practice problems or exercises to gain a better understanding of nonmathematical topics, such as project management, semantics, biomechanics, organic compounds, or immigration, certainly will come as a welcome surprise.

--Encyclopedias
In general, encyclopedias contain many aspects of a broad subject and the desired topic will have to be discovered within. Increasingly the publishing world is providing us with encyclopedic treatments of narrower topics and even very, very narrow topics. We can take comfort knowing that there is something out there for everyone's taste and interest. Find out all about death, jazz, Faulkner, the nineteen seventies, Catholics, mammals, and so on. **Burial and encyclopedias** will delight the true aficionado by unearthing *James Dean in death: A popular encyclopedia of a celebrity phenomenon.*

--Essence, genius, nature
Religions remain popular subjects to explore, and here too we first look for explanations of the central elements. To gain an understanding of religions, this probably little-known subdivision comes to our salvation. These examples of search results with **Judaism, Islam, Buddhism,** or **Christianity** will make you want to check this subdivision in your own catalog.

Down-to-earth Judaism: Food, money, sex, and the rest of life

Bridge to light: Spiritual wayfaring towards Islam

Happiness and immortality: George Grimm's investigation into the secrets of Buddhism

The faith: What Christians believe, why they believe it, and why it matters

--Miscellanea

Still have some questions about a topic? **--Miscellanea** will supply works in the Q&A format. It will also get you in touch with some of the more obscure facts or a very special aspect of a topic. Philosophy, law, or Islam still has you perplexed? Get further enlightenment with a **--Miscellanea** search.

Eureka! What Archimedes really meant and 80 other key ideas explained

Nolo's encyclopedia of everyday law: Answers to your most frequently asked legal questions

Responses to 101 questions on Islam

CHAPTER 2

FINDING HOW-TO GUIDES

BEST ALL-AROUND

--Amateur's manuals
The best of the how-to subdivisions. **--Amateur's manuals** is paired with technical topics (e.g., carpentry, photography, website design, beer brewing). The topics can be very technical (and probably not for true amateurs), such as electrical wiring!

--Technique
Want to know how to do it, step by step? **--Technique** finds "nontheoretical works describing steps to be followed in performing required tasks" (Library of Congress 2008a, H1095). Covers all disciplines, but is weighted toward the lab sciences and artistic endeavors.

> *Observing comets, asteroids, meteors, and the zodiacal light*
> *Basic drafting for interior designers*
> *Bodyworks: A visual guide to drawing the figure*
> *Ice carving made easy*
> *The joy of dancing: The next steps: Ballroom, Latin and jive for social dancers of all ages*

--Handbooks, manuals, etc.
Intended for the "when in doubt, read the directions" crowd. Handbooks and manuals are often more in-depth than a dictionary or encyclopedia entry and are great for professionals and amateurs who want to understand a topic.

> *Making your money work for you: How to use simple investment principles to increase your wealth*

Golfer's start-up
Caring for your own dead

🔍 **MAGIC SEARCH:** [topic of interest] and (manuals or technique). Pulls in all three subdivisions, thus a plethora of how-to guides!

--Vocational guidance
Sounds like a real snoozer, but it comes to the rescue when you really need it! How do I find a job in medical anthropology? Fashion design? Just how do I go about becoming a rock star?

⊕ **BONUS FEATURE:** These books often get to the nitty-gritty of how to dress for an interview, how to write a résumé—how to say, "Look out world, here I come!"

HOW TO DO IT YOURSELF

--Design and construction
--Design
--Designs and plans

> **--Design and construction** goes with "structures, machines, equipment, etc." (Library of Congress 2008a, H1532). This subdivision finds materials on how something was built (e.g., a sixteenth-century Turkish mosque) or how to build something today (e.g., a fountain). There are lots of do-it-yourself items here (imagine the bookshelf at your local home-improvement store), but some titles, such as *Aerospace design,* are not for rookies!

> **--Design** goes with topics that are not constructed, such as gardens, book jackets, running shoes, and quilts.

> **--Designs and plans,** which goes with resources that contain "architectural drawings" (Library of Congress 2008a, H1532), will be helpful for those interested in home or landscape improvement, whether they want to browse and dream or are ready to build.

Library of Congress makes a fine distinction between **--Design** and **--Design and construction.** Try instead the following:

🔍 **MAGIC SEARCH:** [your interest] and design*

--Maintenance and repair
How to take care of and fix anything that requires maintenance and repair (e.g., your water heater, your airplane, your harpsichord).

--Repairing
Goes with things that the Library of Congress has decided do not require maintenance! (Library of Congress 2008a, H1095): clothing, jewelry, and furniture. This comes as a surprise to anyone who has done tedious housework, but try our no-fuss search:

⭐ **MAGIC SEARCH:** [your how-to interest] and repair*

HOW TO TEACH YOURSELF . . .

Anything

--Textbooks
Textbooks, according to Cataloger's Desktop, are "presented in a simplified manner [and are] explicitly intended to be used for the purpose of learning [a] subject" (Library of Congress 2008a, H2187). Though they are usually used in the classroom, textbooks can be a handy way to read up on or review a topic (e.g., calculus, public speaking, thermodynamics!). Many books have activities included to help you learn.

ⓘ **NOTE: --Textbooks** was very narrowly defined until 2002.

--Study and teaching
How to teach or study any topic. Many are written for teachers of young people (*Kids' poems: Teaching kindergartners to love writing poetry*), but some are more like textbooks. These often feature hands-on activities. This is not the most perfect how-to, but it goes with so many different topics that it is worthy of an honorable mention.

Music

--Instruction and study
Pitch perfect for music teachers and students, as this is for music topics and only music topics.

> *Playing the violin*
> *Learn to yodel*
> *How to teach music to children*

--Self-instruction
Use with musical instruments. This subdivision is just right for the bashful person, scared to sign up for a class. And because there are many of us who could never learn how to fiddle on our own, you may get better hits with **--Instruction and study!** Find jewels like *Mel Bay presents clawhammer banjo from scratch.*

⭐ **MAGIC SEARCH:** [your musical interest] and (instruction or self-instruction)

A Language

A quick path to the pleasures of learning another language. Find audio and visual materials as well as books.

--Textbooks for foreign speakers
Avoids a German textbook written completely in German, for native speakers of German, for instance. Find a wide range of titles, from basic (*Let's study Urdu: An introductory course*) to advanced materials (*Tell it like it is! Natural Chinese for advanced learners*).

--Self-instruction
Traveling to an exotic locale this summer? Learn on your own by using a book or listening to CDs in your car.

> *Beginner's Russian grammar*
> *The complete idiot's guide to learning French*

HOW TO REVIEW

You already know it; you just need to brush up—probably for a big test! And a good way to do that? Practice, practice, practice!

--Study guides
Often handy for graduate and professional exam preparation, and the results can include practice questions and problems.

--Examinations, questions, etc.
Titles generally provide practice questions (and answers!) for a specific type of exam (e.g., GRE, LSAT).

--Problems, exercises, etc.
Practice activities for any topic from academic writing to X-ray spectroscopy.

Not sure when to use what? We (and possibly a lot of catalogers) aren't either! Because of the exceedingly fine line, we recommend a more comprehensive search:

MAGIC SEARCH: [topic] and (examinations or problems or study guides)

HOW TO TRAVEL

--Guidebooks

How do I get there? Where do I stay? What should I eat? What is there to do? **--Guidebooks** will get you to the answers. Find resources like Rough Guides and Fodor's.

⊕ **BONUS FEATURE:** Find out where to indulge in your hobby (e.g., fishing, hiking, bird-watching, shopping).

--Tours

Very similar to **--Guidebooks**, but with structured itineraries (Library of Congress 2008a, H1645). This is perfect for the traveler who likes a plan. The titles you will discover often have surprising twists.

Hidden New York

Fugitives and refugees: A walk in Portland, Oregon

--Social life and customs

This is a great one for how to behave and act when you are visiting: Do I shake hands? Take my shoes off? Kiss my host? Find titles that describe the customs and habits of people in a certain place.

--Description and travel

No basic guidebooks here; instead, learn what to expect, what other travelers have experienced. You often get a long-ago and faraway glimpse of the place. Academic collections may have resources that are more description and less travel!

CHAPTER 3

FINDING IMAGES

Isn't a picture worth a thousand words? Are certain images not part of our collective memory? Then finding the right one is crucial, and it will be much easier with the help of these subdivisions.

BEST ALL-AROUND

--Pictorial works
Always the first choice for finding images of anything—people, places, things, even processes, ideas, and personal qualities. Even better, **--Pictorial works** is assigned only when "more than 50 [percent] of the work is pictorial" or "the publication features, or stresses the importance of, the illustrations" (Library of Congress 2008a, H1935). Images may be in any medium: photographs, drawings, woodcuts, engravings, and so on.

--Popular works
A good bet, because works written for the layperson are often illustrated. Note one limit: **--Popular works** is assigned only to books in the science disciplines, in technical fields, in medicine, and in law (Library of Congress 2008a, H1943.5).

--Juvenile literature
Don't be put off by the tag *juvenile*! This subdivision leads to excellent images fit for any age group. Think of the crystal-clear photographs in Dorling Kindersley (DK) books, for example, or the detailed drawings in David Macaulay's *Cathedral*!

--Charts, diagrams, etc.
This subdivision rates a best all-around because of the nature of its illustrations rather than for its frequency of use. **--Charts, diagrams, etc.** yields

graphic representations that can clarify a topic or provide ideas for that big presentation. **Stocks and charts, diagrams** finds *The Wall Street waltz: 90 visual perspectives;* **mythology and charts, diagrams** gets *A genealogical chart of Greek mythology.* Who would have thought?

--In art
Always artistic but not always Rembrandt. **--In art** finds books with art reproductions that "depict a particular theme" or place (Library of Congress 2008a, H1935). **Project Apollo and in art** yields *Eyewitness to space: Paintings and drawings related to the Apollo mission to the moon.*

> ⊙ **NOTE:** The Library of Congress addresses artistic representations of topics a second way, by creating a set of main headings that pair the topic with the phrase "in art": politics in art, advertising in art, etc.

IMAGES OF PEOPLE, REAL AND MYTHICAL

--Pictorial works
The first choice, every time.

--Portraits
The Library of Congress defines this much more broadly than might the National Portrait Gallery, so expect more than seated heads of state and Elizabethan ruff collars. You'll find images of all kinds of people, from teenage boys (*Coming of age: Photographs by Will McBride*) to country-western singers (*Nashville portraits*). You'll find images of individuals, too, be they living legends or long-dead monarchs.

> ⊘ **RULE:** For the *very long* dead, remember the Rule of A.D. 1400: For persons living before A.D. 1400, **--Art** is used instead (Library of Congress 2008a, H1110). Napoleon, who died in 1821, gets **--Portraits**, while Alexander the Great, who died in 323 B.C., gets **--Art**.

> ⊛ **MAGIC SEARCH:** [individual or group] and (pictorial works or portraits)

--Caricatures and cartoons
Add this one to your search to get the visual essence of an individual or group. Caricaturists go after everyone, from preachers (*There's no business like soul business,* by the late Doug Marlette) to celebrities (*Rolling Stone: The illustrated portraits*).

IMAGES OF PLACES

--Pictorial works
Always!

--Description and travel

The most widely used subdivision for places, this one is for works that describe a place or that present accounts of travel in that place. Results are usually illustrated.

--Guidebooks
--Tours

Ignore the rules that tell catalogers how to decide between **--Guidebooks** and **--Tours**. If you want pictures of a place, use them both.

✦ **MAGIC SEARCH:** [place] and (pictorial works or guidebooks or tours or description)

--Discovery and exploration
--Early accounts to 1600
--Early works to 1800

Books described by these subdivisions have illustrations that are one of a kind. Well-funded exploring parties of the fifteenth to seventeenth centuries always included an artist, and later expeditions took along photographers. Find their accounts, and you will see the earliest visual records of a place.

✓ **RULES:**

--**Discovery and exploration** is only for those places "that are unsettled or sparsely settled and are unknown to the rest of the world" (Library of Congress 2008a, H1564).

--**Early accounts to 1600** is limited to the Americas.

--**Early works to 1800** is based entirely on the date the work was created.

✦ **MAGIC SEARCH:** [place-name] and (early works or early accounts or discovery)

--Aerial photographs
--Photographs from space

Provide an unusual perspective on a surprisingly wide range of places.

Parks and gardens of Britain: A landscape history from the air
The Appalachian Trail: An aerial view

There are even ancient places aerially rendered:

Egypt: Antiquities from above

IMAGES OF OBJECTS

--Pictorial works
Obviously!

Five "collections" subdivisions

Books about collecting things are heavily illustrated, and the quality of the images is usually high. Library of Congress has defined these subdivisions with impressive granularity, with one assigned to natural objects, another to man-made items, and yet another to things that can be preserved (as well as collected!). Some subdivisions must be tied to the owner of the collection; others go with the object collected. Rather than attempt to untie this Gordian knot, we recommend a sharp cut with the following:

MAGIC SEARCH: [research interest] and (collect* or catalogs or exhibitions)

 --Catalogs. For "types of merchandise, art objects, collectors' items, technical equipment" (Library of Congress 2008a, H1360).

--Catalogs and collections. For natural objects and musical instruments (Library of Congress 2008a, H1360). (Only those two categories! What was the Library of Congress thinking?)

--Collectors and collecting. "For types of objects, *excluding* natural objects" (Library of Congress 2008a, H1095).

--Collection and preservation. Useful for pictures of mummies, insects, automobiles, and any other object that can be collected *and* preserved.

--Exhibitions. Most often used for topics in art, but **--Exhibitions** also pops up with livestock (think county fairs) and technological innovations (Chicago World's Fair and the Ferris wheel).

Also retrieved by the Magic Search, thank goodness: **--Archaeological collections, --Art collections, --Bonsai collections, --Coin collections, --Ethnological collections, --Ethnomusicological collections, --Map collections, --Musical instrument collections, --Natural history collections, --Numismatic collections, --Photograph collections, --Poster collections, --Private collections, --Scientific apparatus collections, --Slide collections, --Stamp collections.**

--Design
--Design and construction
--Designs and plans
See clear illustrations of fountains, garages, robots, floor plans, electric cars, walking trails—anything a person can design and/or build!

MAGIC SEARCH: [object] and (design*)

--Atlases
All images, all the time, but with one condition: the object must fall into the realm of the scientific, the technical, or the medical (Library of Congress 2008a, H1935). Lightning, root canals, chickens, and sewage can have **--Atlases**. Expect brutally graphic photographs.

--Guidebooks

Niche travel means that every special interest has its guidebook! So, **theaters and guidebooks, castles and guidebooks, battlefields and guidebooks, gardens and guidebooks,** and on and on and on.

--Identification

Have an unidentified found object? A rock, a shell, a mushroom, perhaps? Try this subdivision, commonly assigned to field guides to the natural world. Fair warning to the fainthearted: human remains, too.

--Specifications

The Library of Congress says it best: "detailed descriptions . . . for a proposed building, structure, product, etc." (Library of Congress 2008a, H2083). This can mean bottles, bolts, buildings, food additives, pistols, trucks, bridges— or eighteenth-century French handkerchiefs!

YOU WOULD THINK, BUT YOU MIGHT BE MISLED— AND THEN AGAIN, MAYBE JUST RIGHT

Why didn't --**Illustrations** and --**Photographs** make the list? Library of Congress instructs us to think of these subdivisions in a very narrow way.

--**Photographs** leads to actual photographs, that is, individual photographic prints or digital photographs of the type housed in archives or special collections.

--**Illustrations** is limited to collections of pictorial representations of individual works, sacred works, individual literatures, literary forms, and "types of published materials" (Library of Congress 2008a, H1659). Combine it with a person's name and you will get pictorial representations of a person's written works, not a picture of the person!

CHAPTER 4

WORDS, WORDS, . . . AND NUMBERS

Words, words, mere words, no matter from the heart.

Shakespeare

DESCRIPTIONS OF WORDS

--Dictionaries

For definitions, **--Dictionaries** should be your first stop. The Library of Congress defines **--Dictionaries** just as we would, as "comprehensive, alphabetical lists [of terms] . . . usually with definitions" (Library of Congress 2008a, H1540). In addition to basic language dictionaries, this subdivision serves up a feast of subject dictionaries. Some sample titles will give you a taste.

Muckrakers: A biographical dictionary of writers and editors

Love, sex, and marriage: A historical thesaurus

Essential terms of fashion: A collection of definitions

An Arabic-English lexicon

⊕ **BONUS FEATURE:** You know those items that are really dictionaries, but have *encyclopedia* or *thesaurus* in the title? Don't worry, your catalogers are on top of it and assign **--Dictionaries** to help avoid confusion.

The Not-Quite Dictionaries

Dictionaries are complete and alphabetical as a rule, so the Library of Congress has developed other subdivisions for lists of definitions that are not necessarily comprehensive or in alphabetical order. These are their stories.

--Terminology. The most inclusive option other than **--Dictionaries**, **--Terminology** describes "works that list or discuss words and expressions" (Library of Congress 2008a, H1095) used in a particular setting or scholarly discipline.

A glossary of literary terms

Perfect phrases for sales and marketing copy

Dictionary of energy and fuels

--Glossaries, vocabularies, etc.
--Vocabulary
--Conversation and phrase books
All go with languages and are great for building one's vocabulary.

> **--Glossaries, vocabularies, etc.** "For incomplete lists of the words of a language [which may or may not be alphabetically arranged], with or without definitions" (Library of Congress 2008a, H2184).
>
> > *A vocabulary, English and Greek: Arranged systematically, to advance the learner in scientific, as well as verbal knowledge*
> >
> > *The joys of Yiddish; a relaxed lexicon of Yiddish, Hebrew and Yinglish words often encountered in English . . . from the days of the Bible to those of the beatnik*
> >
> > *1500+ keywords for $100,000+ jobs*
>
> Use also **--Vocabulary**, which, according to Library of Congress, should be paired with "languages other than English" (Library of Congress 2008a, H1154). It almost always overlaps with **--Glossaries, vocabularies, etc.**, which covers all languages.

⊙ **RECOMMENDATION:** The Library of Congress should move to one subdivision for all languages: **--Glossaries, vocabularies, etc.**

> **--Conversation and phrase books.** Handy for world travelers and for people who need to speak a foreign language in a professional setting.
>
> > *Focus on contemporary Arabic*
> >
> > *Survival Spanish for pharmacists*
> >
> > *How to say "fabulous!" in 8 different languages: A travel phrase book for gay men*

🔍 **MAGIC SEARCH:** [language] and (glossaries or vocabulary or phrase)

--Nomenclature
Used with "scientific and technical disciplines . . . for systematically derived lists of names or designations that have been formally adopted or sanctioned, or for discussions of the principles involved in the creation and application of such names" (Library of Congress 2008a, H1095).

> *Dictionary of plant lore*
>
> *Birds of the world: Recommended English names*
>
> *Snakes of the Americas: Checklist and lexicon*
>
> *This is not a weasel: A close look at nature's most confusing terms*

--Gazetteers
For tracking down information about places. The Library of Congress defines a gazetteer as "a geographical dictionary in which names of places are given in alphabetical order with location and/or coordinates. In addition, entries sometimes include pronunciation and brief historical information" (Library of Congress 2008a, H1630).

--Abbreviations
--Acronyms
What does RDA or AWOL or ALA mean? **--Abbreviations** and **--Acronyms** lead to sources that will spell things out for you!

> *Acrosport: Acronyms used for sport, physical education and recreation*
> *Music abbreviations: A reverse dictionary*
> *Dictionary of medical acronyms and abbreviations*

We are grateful that the Library of Congress didn't create a third subdivision, to cover initialisms, but still we offer this:

⊘ **RECOMMENDATION:** Because most dictionaries of this type include both abbreviations and acronyms under one cover, the Library of Congress should create the all-encompassing subdivision, **--Abbreviations, acronyms, etc.**, ASAP! Until the Library of Congress combines these, use this:

⊛ **MAGIC SEARCH:** [area of interest] and (abbreviations or acronyms)

WORDS FOR WORDSMITHS

--Synonyms and antonyms
Library of Congress uses **--Dictionaries** for dictionaries but uses **--Synonyms and antonyms** instead of *thesauri*.

> *Using French synonyms*
> *Vox: Diccionario de sinónimos*
> *Roget's 21st century thesaurus*
> *Oxford dictionary of synonyms and antonyms*

--Reverse indexes
Oh, what's the word for _____? Try **--Reverse indexes** to find out!

> *The inverted medical dictionary: A method of finding medical terms*
> *   quickly*
> *-Ologies and -isms: A thematic dictionary*

Reader's Digest reverse dictionary: How to find the words on the tip of your tongue

--Homonyms

Books of homonyms are often humorous, but the serious ones will keep a writer from talking about a "wicker receptacle for carrying sacred utensils in ancient Rome" (a cist) when he means to talk about a cyst, "an abnormal closed sac in a body" (Hobbs 1999, 62).

Look-alike, sound-alike, not-alike words: An index of confusables

Homographs: Bow and bow and other words that look the same but sound as different as sow and sow

(!) **NOTE:** Homophones seem to be included with homonyms (*A chocolate moose for dinner*).

EXPRESSIONS

These subdivisions usually lead to lists that will help you express yourself, as well as lists of words and phrases to avoid! Expect also to find resources that talk about the concepts of idioms, slang, and so on.

--Terms and phrases

This subdivision seems to be a catchall. Its purpose is to locate resources "that list or discuss expressions, phrases, etc., found in" a language (Library of Congress 2008b, sh 85134037). The key distinction between **--Terms and phrases** and **--Glossaries, vocabularies, etc.** and other dictionary types is "expressions, phrases" rather than simply lists of words. This overlaps considerably with more specialized terms like **--Idioms, --Jargon**, and **--Slang**.

Bugaboos, chimeras and Achilles' heels: 10,001 difficult words and how to use them

Chinese sayings

--Idioms

According to the inside cover of the *Longman dictionary of English idioms,* an idiom is "a fixed group of words with a different meaning from the meanings of the separate words" (Long 1979, 88). Examples from the Longman collection include "dressed to kill" and "paint the town red" (Long 1979).

What's up? A guide to American collegespeak

A dictionary of Russian idioms and colloquialisms: 2,200 expressions with examples

In a pickle, and other funny idioms

--Slang

> *The new Partridge dictionary of slang and unconventional English*
>
> *Street French: How to speak and understand French slang; A self-teaching guide*
>
> *Dictionary of sexual slang: Words, phrases, and idioms from AC/DC to zig-zig*

--Jargon

This absurdly long title says it all: *Green weenies and due diligence: Insider business jargon—raw, serious and sometimes funny business and deal terms from an entrepreneur's diary that you won't get from school or a dictionary.* **Consider also** --Government jargon!

--Euphemism

If you don't have anything nice to say, try saying it this way! Note the singular form.

> *How not to say what you mean: A dictionary of euphemisms*
>
> *Kind words: A thesaurus of euphemisms*

--Obscene words

To avoid or enjoy!

> *Expletive deleted: A good look at bad language*

WORDS OF WISDOM

--Quotations
--Quotations, maxims, etc.

Both provide compilations of carefully chosen quotes.

> **--Quotations**. Goes with groups of people or individuals (sometimes fictional!).
>
> > *The words of Desmond Tutu*
> >
> > *People on people: The Oxford dictionary of biographical quotations*
> >
> > *The wisdom of the Native Americans*

Consider also --Language--Glossaries, etc., "terms used in the speech or writings of a person" (*Hildegard of Bingen's unknown language*) (Library of Congress 2008a, H1540).

--Quotations, maxims, etc. Used with topics and places.

> *Excellent memorables for all mourners*
>
> *A dictionary of quotations and proverbs about cats and dogs*
>
> *Football coach quotes: The wit, wisdom and winning words of leaders on the gridiron*

Some titles suit both categories. For *The Pooh book of quotations: In which will be found some useful information and sustaining thoughts by Winnie-the-Pooh and his friends,* **--Quotations** is assigned to author A. A. Milne and **--Quotations, maxims, etc.** is assigned to "Teddy bears in literature" and "Winnie-the-Pooh (Fictitious character)"! When in doubt, use this:

⭐ **MAGIC SEARCH: [research interest or person/group] and quotations**
And, while we're at it:

☺ **RECOMMENDATION:** The Library of Congress should let **--Quotations, maxims, etc.** serve everyone and everything!

WORD HISTORY

--Etymology
Explore the history of words by finding items like the classic *Oxford English Dictionary.*

> *Nouveau dictionnaire étymologique et historique*
>
> *Inventing English: A portable history of the language*
>
> *The life of language: The fascinating ways words are born, live and die*

--New words

> *Clichés and coinages*
>
> *The official dictionary of unofficial English: A crunk omnibus for thrillionaires and bampots for the Ecozoic Age*

--Obsolete words
Gone but not forgotten, thanks to this subdivision.

> *Dewdroppers, waldos, and slackers: A decade-by-decade guide to the vanishing vocabulary of the twentieth century*
>
> *Poplollies and bellibones: A celebration of lost words*

--Lexicography
According to Merriam-Webster Online (www.merriam-webster.com), lexicography is "the editing or making of a dictionary." Read about the process, which can be surprisingly interesting!

*The dumb linguists: A study of the earliest English and Dutch
   dictionaries*

*The professor and the madman: A tale of murder, insanity, and the
   making of the Oxford English Dictionary*

NUMBERS

--Mathematics

Like it or not, math is all around and not easily avoided. **--Mathematics** either
explores how math is used in a great variety of fields or explains the mathematical systems used by ethnic groups.

Culinary math

Fundamental mathematics of life insurance

or

Maori mathematics: Traditional measurement

Mathematics of the Incas: Code of the Quipu

--Tables

Indeed, these true time-savers provide "results already computed, worked
out, or processed" (Library of Congress 2008a, H2160).

Food composition and nutrition tables

*Consumer credit computation and compliance guide with annual
   percentage rate tables*

--Conversion tables

No need to remember complicated conversion formulae; whether for calendars, measurements, money, temperature, or time—it's all ready to go!

A guide to international measurements

*The Muslim and Christian calendars: Being tables for the conversion of
   Muslim and Christian dates from the Hijra to the year A.D. 2000*

--Statistics

"Facts are stubborn things, but statistics are more pliable," according to
Mark Twain. The truth is, numerical data—collected, analyzed, interpreted
or explained—tell important stories in a unique way.

--Statistical methods

Learn more about the "methods of compiling, studying, and using statistics,"
or "for discussions of the methods of solving problems on . . . topics through
the use of statistics" (Library of Congress 2008a, H2095).

Baseball by the numbers: How statistics are collected, what they mean,
and how they reveal the game

--Observations

This leads to "numerical data obtained by the observation of natural phenomena or for discussions on the processing and use of those data" (Library
of Congress 2008a, H1095).

Radar observation of clear air and clouds
Manual for analysis of rodent populations

CHAPTER 5

FINDING OUT ABOUT PEOPLE
Individuals and Groups

Often research requires gathering information about specific individuals or groups of people, but there's a catch.

Library of Congress has three lists of subdivisions that go with people: the "Names of Persons" list, for individuals; the "Classes of Persons" list, for groups like motorcyclists, impressionists, and older people; and the "Ethnic Groups" list. Some subdivisions appear in all three lists, but many do not. That means that not all subdivisions can be attached to individuals (e.g., **--Biography** is not assigned to individuals)! And not all subdivisions go with groups (e.g., only individuals can have **--Aesthetics**). Again, here we are confronted with rules, rules, rules.

And here's where we give you permission to ignore all that!

No worries! The keyword search strategy allows us to take advantage of all the "people" subdivisions without worrying too much whether they come from the **Name**, the **Class**, or the **Ethnic** list. In the following entries we mention the rules only when they really matter, and, as usual, we give you Magic Searches to help along the way!

LIFE EVENTS

--Childhood and youth

A rich subdivision, as it must be, given that it covers toddlerdom through the teenage years. Who knew Ralph Nader even had a childhood? But *The seventeen traditions,* by Nader himself, reveals how he became the man he is. *Young Stalin* tells the story of a "nondescript peasant boy" with an "overprotective mother" and a shoemaker father (*Publisher's Weekly,* 2007). The Library of Congress also provides us **--Pre-existence** and **--Birth**, but results are limited. The former is mostly for the Buddha and Jesus Christ (no Shirley

MacLaine!). And though *videos* of people's births were wildly popular in the 1980s, few people took the time to write a whole book about the event.

--Marriage
--Divorce
Bring books about legendary couples such as Queen Victoria and Albert, Prince Consort, and about well-known figures whose lives are fully documented: Charles Lindbergh, Leo Tolstoy, Henry VIII.
See also **--Family** for some of the juicier tales of pairs.

--Last years
--Last years and death
The Library of Congress goes straight from marriage and divorce to the near end, shortchanging adulthood in the process (try the section "What They Did" in this chapter for those years). Like many of the other "Life Events" subdivisions, **--Last years** is most useful when a search for the person's name alone is likely to yield too many hits.

> *Voltaire in exile: The last years, 1753-78*
>
> *The long, slow death of Jack Kerouac* (Is it the "long" and "slow" aspect that puts this in the **--Last years** category rather than in **--Death and burial?**)
>
> *Late Beethoven: Music, thought, imagination*

--Death and burial (for individuals)
--Death (for groups)
These seem an obvious choice for the researcher interested in end of life, but a search on **[person's name] and death and burial** will miss the many works tagged with **--Last years**. And numerous searches suggest that catalogers rarely assign both **--Death and burial** and **--Last years** to a book. No matter that death and burial typically occur in one's last years or that one's last years usually conclude with death and burial! The comprehensive thanatologist is advised to use this:

⊛ **MAGIC SEARCH: [person's name] and (death or last years)**

--Biography
This is a "wouldn't you think?" subdivision for sure, as in "wouldn't you think **--Biography** would show up in every biography's catalog record?" Think again! Library of Congress reserves **--Biography** for groups of people and does not allow it to be attached to an individual's name! A biography of Elvis Presley would have as its subject heading **Presley, Elvis, 1935-1977**, with no **--Biography** attached. So adding "biography" to a search actually *eliminates* many bona fide biographies from the search results.

⊛ **MAGIC SEARCH:** just **Presley, Elvis**

⊙ **NOTE** (for motivated readers only): Until 1998, the Library of Congress rules told catalogers to attach **--Biography** to individuals in one group: *literary* authors. Your own catalog might still have some records from that time. This might look like a great opportunity for a catalog cleanup, but what would you gain from such a project? Leave well enough alone. In fact:

⊚ **RECOMMENDATION:** The Library of Congress should authorize the use of **--Biography** for individuals. And we mean *all* individuals.

WHAT THEY DID

--Books and reading

George Herbert (1593–1633) expressed the opinion: "Woe be to him that reads but one book." To find out about a person's reading habits and interests, **--Books and reading** comes to the rescue. Lists of books recommended for or read by groups or individuals are assigned **--Books and reading**, too, and further subdivided by **--Bibliography**. No need to fear George Herbert's pity any longer.

> *"The tools of my trade": The annotated books in Jack London's library*
> *The Harvard guide to influential books: 113 distinguished Harvard*
>   *professors discuss the books that have helped to shape their thinking*
> *Theodore Roosevelt, the making of a conservationist*

--Knowledge and learning

Where did an individual learn all that he or she seems to know? The expected search term might be **--Education**, but alas, that is used only with groups. Instead, **--Knowledge and learning** covers this territory, whether the scholarly pursuit was formal or informal. The learning of a specific topic or the knowledge of a specific topic is covered by **--Knowledge--[topic]**.

> *Watershed at Leavenworth: Dwight D. Eisenhower and the Command*
>   *and General Staff School*
> *The education of Le Corbusier*
> *How to be an intellectual in the age of TV: The lessons of Gore Vidal*

⊚ **RECOMMENDATION:** Let not a fine distinction prevent information seekers from finding what they are looking for. Classes of persons receive **--Education**; ethnic groups receive **--Education**; individuals acquire **--Knowledge and learning**? The Library of Congress should decide between

--**Knowledge and learning** and --**Education** and use the same subdivision in all cases.

--Literary art

Discussions of the literary accomplishments and abilities of nonliterary notables are grouped under --**Literary art**. William Jennings Bryan, Abraham Lincoln, and Winston Churchill deservedly will have this subdivision attached to their names.

--Contributions in

"For works discussing the person's actual substantive contributions or accomplishments in a specific field or topic, whether made as a result of a vocation or an avocation. . . . Also . . . for works discussing the person's philosophy or system of thought that he or she propounded or imparted to others" (Library of Congress 2008a, H1110). Results affirm (Enrico Fermi's --**Contributions in nuclear physics**), remind that accomplishments expand to associated areas (Frank Lloyd Wright's --**Contributions in furniture design**), and surprise (Vladimir Nabokov's --**Contributions in entomology**).

--Performances

Compiles works about the performances of dancers, singers, performers of all types, as well as works about the performances of works by composers and choreographers.

> *Luciano Pavarotti: The myth of the tenor*
>
> *Verdi at the Golden Gate: Opera and San Francisco in the gold rush years*

--Appreciation

For most creative people, just doing it isn't enough. Their work must be seen and appreciated. This subdivision presents works on the "public response and reception, praise, etc., of the person's artistic or literary works" (Library of Congress 2008a, H1110).

> *The reception of Blake in the Orient*
>
> *A monumental vision: The sculpture of Henry Moore*
>
> *Charles Dickens in cyberspace*
>
> *Growing up with Audrey Hepburn*
>
> *Milton and the rabbis*

--Employment

Breaking the bamboo ceiling; How to save the underclass; Pride against prejudice—what could these titles have in common? All three deal with

--Employment of groups of people: Asian Americans, men, and Puerto Ricans, respectively.

--Political activity

Political participation includes protesting, lobbying, trying to persuade others "to do what needs to done" for a better world. These activities by individuals and groups of people give insight into real or perceived injustices and the struggles to improve conditions. **--Political activity** reminds us of relatively recent historical events in our own country, with titles such as

> *The case of Joe Hill*
>
> *Red star over Hollywood: The film colony's long romance with the left*
>
> *Soldiers in revolt: GI resistance during the Vietnam War*

(!) **NOTE:** For political activity by ethnic groups or individual members of an ethnic group, use instead **--Politics and government**.

--Trials, litigation, etc.

Sometimes justice is called into action to resolve conflicts in a person's life. **--Trials, litigation, etc.** is used for the official proceedings of a trial or for works about a trial in which the person was either the defendant (criminal trials) or a party (civil trials) (Library of Congress 2008a, H2228).

> *The trial of Galileo*
>
> *Dred Scott and the politics of slavery*
>
> *The Mary Ellen Wilson child abuse case and the beginning of children's rights in 19th century America*

--Captivity or --Imprisonment

Being involuntarily confined falls into either **--Captivity** or **--Imprisonment**. The time a person spent as a captive, whether under house arrest or as a hostage, calls for **--Captivity** (Library of Congress 2008a, H1078), as in *Narrative of the captivity and sufferings of Mrs. Hannah Lewis, and her three children*. **--Imprisonment** recalls time spent in a "correctional institution or a prisoner-of-war camp" (Library of Congress 2008a, H1110).

--Recreation

All work and no play make anybody ready for some R&R. **--Recreation** fills us in as to which recreational activities groups like to engage in. It also tells us which recreational activities would benefit us most, according to the experts.

> *Keeping busy: A handbook of activities for persons with dementia*
>
> *The recreational pursuits and health habits of long-distance truck drivers*

--Travel
On the road again, but not necessarily as a long-distance truck driver. **--Travel** leads us to accounts of journeys related to us by the traveler or by others.

> *Seductive journey: American tourists in France from Jefferson to the Jazz Age*
>
> *Humboldt's cosmos: Alexander von Humboldt and the Latin American journey that changed the way we see the world*
>
> *The journal of a tour to the Hebrides, with Samuel Johnson, LL.D.*
>
> *Smile when you're lying: Confessions of a rogue travel writer*

--Alcohol use, --Drug use, --Substance use, --Tobacco use
Recreational activities or vices? or, Who uses or abuses what?

> *The chemically dependent nurse*
>
> *Spitting into the wind: The facts about dip and chew* **(athletes and tobacco use)**
>
> *Pumped: Straight facts for athletes about drugs, supplements, and training*

--Sexual behavior
No further explanation is needed—actors, Bill Clinton, girls, pirates, Zuni Indians—all are covered.

--Spurious and doubtful works
Shakespeare is the winner in the **--Spurious and doubtful works** category. A substantial number of titles are ascribed to Shakespeare, and he generates lots of discussions about works that are attributed to him.

WHAT THEY THOUGHT

--Attitudes
A particular group's (e.g., gay artists, clergy, Russian authors, theater audiences, stepmothers) views on any topic. For what the public thinks about that group, use **--Public opinion.**

--Philosophy
An individual's "personal philosophy" (Library of Congress 2008a, H1110). These are often a person's general thoughts about life, such as *Saving graces: Finding solace and strength from friends and strangers* by Elizabeth Edwards.

ⓘ **NOTE:** **--Philosophy** is not used under actual philosophers.

--Sources

Inspiration may make up only 1 percent of genius, if Thomas Edison is right, but it merits a subdivision! **--Sources** is used "for collections of materials that served as the person's sources of ideas or inspiration for his or her endeavors or creative works, and for discussions of those source materials" (Library of Congress 2008a, H1110). Researchers may have to sweat a bit to find the subdivision used this way in the long lists of primary documents results, but it's worth every drop!

--Views on

"For works discussing the person's opinions or attitudes on a specific topic, whether explicitly stated or inferred" (Library of Congress 2008a, H1110). Readers may get honest insight, as when Elizabeth Taylor explicitly states her **--Views on reducing diets** in *Elizabeth takes off: On weight gain, weight loss, self-image, and self-esteem.* Sometimes anticipation shifts to disappointment, as happens when Keats's **--Views on sex** turns out to be *Sexual power in British romantic poetry.* The rest is all conjecture: at its worst, drivel, and at its best, scholarly speculation.

> *Leisure and lifestyle in selected writings of Karl Marx*
> *Stalin on linguistics and other essays*
> *Eavesdropping in the novel from Austen to Proust*

--Knowledge--[topic]

This will tell you what an individual knows about a specific topic. What did Jane Austen know about anatomy? Shakespeare about sports? Leonardo da Vinci about botany?

--Knowledge and learning

Find out about an individual's "informal learning" in addition to his or her educational background (Library of Congress 2008a, H1110).

> *The imaginative landscape of Christopher Columbus*
> *Arenas of conflict: Milton and the unfettered mind*

⊛ **MAGIC SEARCH: [person] and knowledge**

--Aesthetics

Explains how an individual defines beauty (or art) (Library of Congress 2008a, H1110).

> *The Dickinson sublime*
> *Tragic pleasures: Aristotle on plot and emotion*

--Ethics
Reveals how an individual defines right and wrong.

> *Machiavelli in hell*
> *Machiavelli's virtue*

--Political and social views
Finds items that express an individual's "general" political and social opinions (Library of Congress 2008a, H1110). For their actual activity in the political arena, use **--Political activity**, which also applies to classes of people (Library of Congress 2008a, H1942). For information about ethnic groups and politics, use **--Politics and government.**

--Religion
The religious "beliefs, practices, knowledge, views, etc." of ethnic groups and individuals (excluding theologians) (Library of Congress 2008a, H1997). For classes of people (e.g., coal miners, automobile racing drivers), use **--Religious life.**

THOUGHTS, RECORDED OR REMEMBERED

--Notebooks, sketchbooks, etc.
J. M. W. Turner sketches scenes on the Thames; Kate Chopin records submissions, rejections, and payouts; Steinbeck keeps a diary as he writes *The grapes of wrath;* and Henry James notes tea with Mrs. Wharton on September 23, 1913. **--Notebooks, sketchbooks, etc.** are collections of these bits and pieces, rich sources that allow the reader to watch the artist at work.

--Diaries
"Records of . . . observations, thoughts, or feelings . . . customarily intended for private rather than public use" (Library of Congress 2008a, H1538).

> *The China diary of George H. W. Bush*
> *Kamikaze diaries*
> *The diary of John Wesley Powell: Conquering the Grand Canyon*

--Quotations
For words of wisdom that might not make it into *Bartlett's.*

> *It's not easy being green: And other things to consider,* by Jim Henson, the Muppets, and Friends
> *Wit and wisdom of the founding fathers*

Warren Buffett speaks

Oscar Wilde in quotation: 3,100 insults, anecdotes, and aphorisms

THE WAY THEY WERE

--Psychology

Because the **--Psychology** subdivision includes behavioral aspects and general personality characteristics (Library of Congress 2008a, H1095), it is your best bet for getting down to what makes a person tick. Find a wealth of information about groups of people and ethnic groups (e.g., stepmothers, dog owners, Eskimos). Individuals are included too; a search for **Mike Tyson and psychology** finds *Tyson: Nurture of the beast.*

--Social life and customs

This is an astonishing subdivision—perfect for finding out about a certain group's everyday life.

Growing up Amish: The teenage years

Under the boards: The cultural revolution in basketball

As strong as the mountains: A Kurdish cultural journey

--Conduct of life

Focuses on the "standards of behavior" for a group and often addresses morals and etiquette (Library of Congress 2008b, sh 85030802). Titles can be written for a certain audience. **Women and conduct of life** produces *The joy of doing things badly: A girl's guide to love, life, and foolish bravery.* The subdivision also finds titles *about* a group of people. **Athletes and conduct of life** wins with *Moral callousness as evidenced by trash talking tee shirts.* **Executives and conduct of life** begets *Total leadership: Be a better leader, have a richer life.*

--Economic conditions

Gives you a picture of the economic situation (current or historical) of a certain group. **Artists and economic conditions** answers *Why are artists poor?*

--Social conditions

Describes the social situation (current or past) of a certain group of people. **Cherokee and social conditions** finds *Blood politics: Race, culture, and identity in the Cherokee Nation of Oklahoma.*

--Humor

Can apply to groups of people (ethnic groups, too) and individuals and can be applied three different ways:

About humor *by* the people (person): Mark Twain, country musicians

About the individual's or group's *sense of humor:* women, Puritans!

Humor *at the person's* (or group's) *expense:* lawyers, rednecks

--Health
Any health-related topic about an individual, including "specific diseases" (Library of Congress 2008a, H1110). This is a great way to find personal stories related to health and illness.

> *FDR's body politics: The rhetoric of disability*
>
> *Why I wore lipstick to my mastectomy*
>
> *Breathing for a living: A memoir*

--Health and hygiene
Find out about the general health status and personal care habits of any group of people (e.g., sailors, Aztecs, farmers, college students). Books are often written *for* the specific group, too. To find out how a specific disease affects a particular group, use **--Diseases**.

> *Body drama: Real girls, real bodies, real issues, real answers*
>
> *The college student's guide to eating well on campus*
>
> *Lessons from the damned: Queers, whores, and junkies respond to AIDS*

--Mental health
Find out about the mental health of an individual or a group.

> *The madness of kings: Personal trauma and the fate of nations*
>
> *Living in the dead zone: Janis Joplin and Jim Morrison*
>
> *Hand trembling, frenzy witchcraft, and moth madness: A study of Navajo seizure disorders*

⊛ **MAGIC SEARCH:** [person or group] and (health or diseases)

PEOPLE THEY KNEW

--Family
Although books with this subdivision may cover a person's family tree, they more frequently dig into relationships—how the family worked or didn't. Princess Diana and the House of Windsor (didn't work), Jimmy Carter and his mother (did work), *Kit Carson and his three wives* (did and did not!). **--Family** is very commonly assigned to memoirs. Because the Library of Congress has no subdivision specifically for that popular genre, this use is welcome.

ⓘ **NOTE:** If the inquiry is about how families work rather than about a particular family, use **--Family relationships**, the subdivision for groups of people (e.g., immigrants, older people, soldiers, teenagers).

--Friends and associates

It may be a crowd of two (Muhammad Ali and Howard Cosell, in *Sound and fury*), a few (*Emerson among the eccentrics*), or many (*All Stalin's men*), but no matter the number, everyone described must be "the person's close and immediate contacts, such as companions, co-workers" (Library of Congress 2008a, H1110). The related subdivision **--Employees** gets few hits, and **--Disciples** is used almost entirely with religious figures.

--Adversaries

More specific in relationship than **--Friends and associates**, **--Adversaries** are "contemporaries who opposed the person's point of view or work" (Library of Congress 2008a, H1110). This one is serious business, not assigned lightly. Historical figures predominate—Napoleon (and Lord Nelson), Bill Clinton (and the conservative right), and Thomas Jefferson (and Aaron Burr).

--Relations with men
--Relations with women

The Library of Congress makes it clear. These are "intimate associations" (Library of Congress 2008a, H1110), not the merely "close and immediate" relationships covered by **--Friends and associates** or the involuntary associations of **--Family** (Library of Congress 2008a, H1110).

> *Whistler, women and fashion*
>
> *Einstein in love: A scientific romance*
>
> *Dear senator* (Strom Thurmond)
>
> *Dead man blues* (Jelly Roll Morton)
>
> *Desiring women* (Virginia Woolf and Vita Sackville-West)

--Relations with

This intriguingly open-ended subdivision specifies neither man nor woman, friend nor foe. It could be anybody, or more accurately, any group of people:

> Journalists (George W. Bush, in *Towel snapping the press*)
>
> Seminole Indians (Andrew Jackson, in *In bitterness and tears*)
>
> Valets (Marcel Proust, in *The memoirs of Ernest A. Forssgren*)

--Contemporaries

Covers people who flourished "during the person's life, but [were] not necessarily in close contact with the person" (Library of Congress 2008a, H1110).

The contemporaries may be known to the person (*The boys from Dolores: Fidel Castro's schoolmates from revolution to exile*) or may not be (*Emily Dickinson and her contemporaries*). Search results offer a personal look at the milieu.

--Correspondence

Unlike **--Diaries**, which by the Library of Congress's definition are intended for the diarist only, letters always involve someone else and can reveal the most private moments of the correspondents' relationships.

> *Wallis and Edward: Letters, 1931-1937: The intimate correspondence of the Duke and Duchess of Windsor*
>
> *Cicero, the secrets of his correspondence*

Not sure whether the relationship with people they knew shifted from close to intimate? From merely contemporary to adversarial? Cross those fine lines with the following:

⊛ **MAGIC SEARCH:** [person's name] and (associates or adversaries or contemporaries or relations with)

THINGS THEY HAD

People's belongings don't get a lot of publishing action, and the number of related subdivisions is proportionally low. These few are worth a mention.

--Clothing

This is most common in the world of cultural anthropology, so ethnic groups predominate, but some individual trendsetters turn up, too. A peek into two very different closets with **Elizabeth and clothing** and **Victoria and clothing** reveals *Queen Elizabeth's wardrobe unlock'd: The inventories of the Wardrobe of Robes prepared in July 1600* and Victoria Beckham's *That extra half an inch: Hair, heels and everything in between.*

--Housing
--Homes and haunts
--Dwellings

> **--Housing** would seem the natural choice for finding books about houses, but in fact this subdivision covers only the socioeconomic angle of human shelter. It definitively lacks the warmth of **--Homes and haunts** or the historical and descriptive slant of **--Dwellings**.
>
> **--Homes and haunts.** Glimpses into the homes and hangouts of individuals or groups are gathered under **--Homes and haunts**.
>
>> *Biltmore Estate: The most distinguished private place*
>>
>> *Monet's garden in art*

> *A goodfella's guide to New York: Your personal tour through*
> *the mob's notorious haunts, hair-raising crime scenes, and*
> *infamous hot spots*

--Dwellings. Brings to life the shelters we have built to protect us over the centuries.

> *The Saxon house*
> *Building an igloo*
> *Design like you give a damn: Architectural responses to*
> *humanitarian crisis*

--Collections

Did you know Roy Acuff's musical collection is displayed at Opryland? What did the Texas philanthropist Ima Hogg fancy and collect? Do some Freudian sleuthing and stumble upon *Excavations and their objects: Freud's collection of antiquity*. Who has what kind of collection worthy to be documented for the ages? The Library of Congress very generously offers an array of collections to choose from: **--Art collections, --Bonsai collections, --Catalogs and collections, --Coin collections, --Ethnological collections, --Ethnomusicological collections, --Herbarium, --Library, --Map collections, --Musical instrument collections, --Natural history collections, --Numismatic collections, --Photograph collections, --Private collections, --Scientific apparatus collections, --Stamp collections**. This abundance of choices calls for this:

⊕**MAGIC SEARCH:** [person's name] and collections

--Antiquities

Describes items left behind by ethnic groups. Searching **Indians and antiquities** will return a wealth of information on the belongings of peoples indigenous to the Americas (the Library of Congress continues to use the terminology "Indians of North [or South] America"). It is advised to search also for individual ethnic groups, such as **Mayas and antiquities**. Finally, a search for **[place name] and antiquities** yields the material riches of inhabitants. **Greece and antiquities** shows us *Everyday things in ancient Greece;* **Scotland and antiquities** finds *In search of the Picts.*

THE WAY THEY WERE IMMORTALIZED

After a productive life, people might be remembered in **--Songs and music** or with a **--Death mask**; tribute paid with **--Monuments** or **--Statues**; pilgrimages organized to visit **--Shrines** or **--Tomb/--Tombs**.

--Obituaries gathers collections of obituaries, the most widely used form of noting a person's death and many times including a short biographical account, relating to groups of people.

Not as imposing as a monument or as evocative as a death mask, but perhaps the best evidence of immortality, is **--Influence**, the long-lasting effect a person has on the world. This simple-sounding subdivision is in reality a powerhouse, yielding large numbers of hits in all areas of human endeavor.

Diana, self-interest, and British national identity

Deadhead social science

Shakespeare and youth culture

CHAPTER 6

FINDING OUT ABOUT PLACES

There are places I remember
All my life though some have changed
Some forever, not for better
Some have gone and some remain

The Beatles, "In My Life," Rubber Soul

BEST ALL-AROUND

--Biography
Cities, continents, counties, countries, provinces, regions, states, and so on, all can have **--Biography**. Offers exquisitely drawn portraits of the history, arts, political and social life, or just plain everyday life of a place.

> *Prayin' to be set free: Personal accounts of slavery in Mississippi*
>
> *Auden and Isherwood: The Berlin years*
>
> *Nepali Aama: Portrait of a Nepalese hill woman*

--Gazetteers
Place-names and geographical features, arranged in alphabetical order. A great source to learn all there is to know about a place: the exact location, the dimensions, the topography, physical features (e.g., mountains, waterways), population figures, gross national product, and more. Some are quite specialized, such as *Cambridge street-names: Their origins and associations.*

⊕ **BONUS FEATURE:** Ever wonder what *Machu Picchu* or *Mississippi* really means? **--Gazetteers** can also point the way to stories of the origins and meanings of place names.

--Social life and customs
For a view of established traditions or the present-day life of a place.

> *Bartered brides: Politics, gender, and marriage in an Afghan tribal society*

Up before daylight: Life histories from the Alabama Writers' Project,
    1938-1939

On city streets: Chicago, 1964-2004

--Description and travel

Great for the armchair tourist or for experiencing travel adventures from another century, as well as providing useful information for today's traveler.

Boswell on the grand tour: Italy, Corsica, and France, 1765-1766

Alaska days with John Muir

Africa on six wheels: A semester on safari

--Guidebooks

This subdivision will explain "how to get there and what to see and do" (Library of Congress 2008a, H1645). Frequent updates make it an indispensable tool for the "no surprises, please" traveler.

Wilderness rivers of Manitoba: Journey by canoe through the land
    where the spirit lives

Trekking in the Nepal Himalaya

--Tours

Simplifies planning the next vacation with ready-made trip itineraries; many times these include informative descriptions about what awaits discovery.

Hallowed ground: A walk at Gettysburg

Romewalks

Crossing the heartland: Chicago to Denver

To cast as wide a net as possible use this:

🔍 MAGIC SEARCH: [place] and (description or guidebooks or tours)

--Buildings, structures, etc.

These words evoke images of hard hats, cranes, girders, trucks, and noise. In reality they lead to a city's historic buildings, ethnic neighborhoods, and hidden architectural treasures.

Secret New York: Exploring the city's hidden neighborhoods

Barcelona, the Great Enchantress

Jerusalem: City of longing

--Literary collections

Want to know, really know, a place? Like postcards from friends (if your friends were really good writers), **--Literary collections** adds a personal element to descriptions of places. One example, *Writing Los Angeles: A literary anthology*, illustrates the genre. There are 880 pages, all on LA: the British artist David Hockney's account of his first visit, Norman Mailer's report on John Kennedy at the 1960 Democratic National Convention, essays by Joan Didion, poems by Bertolt Brecht and Randall Jarrell, a novella by Raymond Chandler, excerpts from Simone de Beauvoir's diary, and a William Faulkner short story. Read all this and you won't need to make the trip at all!

--Pictorial works
Never disappoints, as the well-known proverb promises, "a picture is worth a thousand words." Plus, the Library of Congress insists that "more than 50 [percent] of the work is pictorial" (Library of Congress 2008a, H1935) before this subdivision may be applied.

OTHER SUBDIVISIONS USEFUL FOR PLACES

Historical Context
--Antiquities
--Civilization
--Commerce
--Discovery and exploration
--Early accounts to 1600 (for the Americas only)
--Early works to 1800
--Genealogy
--Historical geography
--History
--Politics and government

That's Life
--Economic conditions
--Emigration and immigration
--Ethnic relations
--Intellectual life
--Moral conditions
--Race relations
--Religion
--Religious life and customs
--Social conditions

Just the Facts

--Boundaries
--Geography
--Maps
--Statistics

Honored in Very Special Ways

--In art
--In bookplates
--In literature
--In mass media
--In motion pictures
--In popular culture
--**On postage stamps** (yes, *on*)
--**On television** (yes, *on*)
--**Songs and music**
--**Humor**
--**Anecdotes**

CHAPTER 7

♪♪♪

FINDING CREATIVE TREATMENTS

Stories, Poems, Songs, etc.

Readers often seek a creative treatment of a topic—a novel about the Mafia, a play about dogs. The following ten subdivisions are guaranteed to find works in any designated genre. One approach leads to items that *are* fiction, drama, songs, and the like (primary); the other shows how a topic is creatively represented in art, in motion pictures, in literature, and so on (secondary).

CREATIVE WORKS, PRIMARY

--Fiction
Assigned to collections of short stories (often) and to novels (sometimes), this subdivision is a relative newcomer (January 2001) (Library of Congress 2008a, H1790). Still, it's worth a try, given readers' requests for "a novel about" or "stories about." It is a bit unreliable as well, given the many rules.

⊘RULES:
Assign only to English-language literatures.

Do not attach to "vague or general topics, such as fate, evil . . . interpersonal relations."

Assign only as the subject comes "readily to mind after a superficial review of the work being cataloged" (Library of Congress 2008a, H1790).

--Drama
Has two applications, one of them obvious and the other unexpected. First, it finds plays on a topic, whether they be individually published or collected. Second, **--Drama** brings up movies and television shows, should your library catalog include media collections.

--Poetry

Unlike **--Drama** and **--Songs and music**, with their audiovisual results, **--Poetry** is straightforward, finding only, well, poems. Although some libraries own separately published poems, results usually take the form of collections:

> *The bird-lover's anthology*
>
> *Going under* **(caves and poetry)**

--Literary collections

Finds mixed anthologies (e.g., poetry, plays, essays, and stories). Perfect for the wavering reader who wants it literary but can't settle on a genre. Just right for those whose reading time comes in minutes, not hours. And best of all, **--Literary collections** usually leads to fine writing. Any interest goes, as you can see:

> *Joys of the road: A little anthology in praise of walking*
>
> *Titanica: The disaster of the century in poetry, song, and prose*
>
> *Growing up gay: A literary anthology*

--Parodies, imitations, etc.

Focuses on creativity spawned by creativity, intended sometimes to mock, sometimes to honor. *Alice in Wonderland* not curious enough? Try *Alternative Alices,* an anthology of literary imitations, revisions, and parodies. Jaded by the same old nursery rhymes? Learn new ones from *The inner city Mother Goose.* Salinger's scant output left you wanting more? Read *With love and squalor: 14 writers respond to the work of JD Salinger.*
See also **--Humor** and **--Caricatures and cartoons**.

--Songs and music

Whether the topic be coal mining, immigration, or even the stock market, there will be music. Sometimes you'll find songbooks, as in *Singing the Vietnam blues,* but many results will be recordings, like *Music of the Crusades,* performed by the Early Music Consort of London.

⊘ **RULE:** **--Songs and music** does not go with "dramatic works with music that can be staged" (Library of Congress 2008a, H2075), which means operas, ballets, and musicals, for example, which the Library of Congress designates **--Drama**. **Cats and songs and music** will not get Andrew Lloyd Webber's *Cats,* no matter how many songs the cats sing!

① **NOTE:** If **--History and criticism** is in the subdivision, too, don't expect notes and lyrics. You've found instead a book *about* songs and music about the topic.

--Musical settings
Want to sing your favorite writer, historical figure, saint? **--Musical settings** identifies "musical scores or sound recordings in which writings or words of the person have been set to music" (Library of Congress 2008a, H1110). It goes only with personal names, but just look at the variety: James Joyce, Louisa May Alcott, Saint Francis of Assisi, Edward Lear, Calamity Jane, and D. H. Lawrence, for heaven's sake.

--Pictorial works
This and other image-finding subdivisions certainly lead to creative treatments of topics.
See chapter 3, "Finding Images," for a complete list.

CREATIVE WORKS, SECONDARY

--In art
--In literature
--In motion pictures
The patient researcher will be well served by these subdivisions that lead to books about a topic as presented in creative venues. And though the path to the goodies is longer than with one-step subdivisions, the results are worth the work. **Cleopatra and in literature** produces a solid reading list for fans of the charismatic queen. *Jesus of Hollywood* **(Jesus and in motion pictures)** belies its clever title by devoting pages 307–313 to an authoritative filmography.

⊘**RULES, RULES, RULES!** We must admit the existence of phrase headings, main subject headings that incorporate "in" phrases: politics in art, mothers in motion pictures, death in literature. The Library of Congress prescribes strict rules for deciding between "**--In**" and "**in . . .**" Fortunately, the freewheeling keyword approach to subject searches takes care of such trifles.

CHAPTER 8

FINDING TRUE STORIES
Memoirs, Observations, and Confessions

Looking for accounts of real situations and people? Want to find real-life stories that illustrate intangibles like emotions and personal characteristics? Try these eight subdivisions that promise at least an element of truth.

--Case studies

A top performer, and the inspiration for this chapter. **--Case studies** finds real-life stories about parent-teacher relationships, gangs, women executives, exorcism, amnesia, racketeering, male prostitution in nineteenth-century France, music therapy, and much more. It is also key for finding examples of characteristics and emotions, such as patriotism, kindness, and grief. How is a case study different from an anecdote? The Library of Congress says that a case study must report "recorded instances," moving it a notch above **--Anecdotes** on the ladder of reliability (Library of Congress 2008a, H1350).

--Anecdotes

Combine this subdivision with any topic to find a wide range of "brief narratives" and "true incidents" (Library of Congress 2008a, H1110). Humor is not a requirement, despite the common definition of the word. For instance, the search **happiness and anecdotes** gets the unfunny *The situation is hopeless, but not serious,* a book about "the pursuit of unhappiness."

--Interviews

Hear it from the horse's mouth. A quick search found collections of interviews with neuroscientists, set designers, stripteasers, and successful people (a real Library of Congress subject heading!). Who could doubt the truth of their stories?

--Personal narratives

Another standout! This subdivision is used for "collective or individual eyewitness reports and/or autobiographical accounts" (Library of Congress 2008a, H1928). Add it to your search vocabulary; it will bring lots of good hits.

> *His affair*
>
> *In the shadow of the Ayatollah: A CIA hostage in Iran*

--Biography

Everyone knows what to expect from this subdivision—life stories—and it does deliver those. But complicated Library of Congress rules mean that **--Biography** works best when paired with groups of people: football players, rock musicians, and missionaries, for example. If you want the biography of an individual, it is best to do a simple subject search on the person's name.

Given the similarities among these subdivisions, it's time for this:

MAGIC SEARCH: [research interest or person] and (anecdotes or interviews or case studies or personal narratives or biography)

--Correspondence

In the past, firsthand accounts of actual events often came in the form of letters, and the Library of Congress has chosen the term **--Correspondence** to describe the format.

--Diaries

Diaries are the most delicious of true stories, and they're a great way to get the inside scoop! Because diaries are "kept daily or at frequent intervals" (Library of Congress 2008a, H1538), they serve as a window into the everyday aspects of life, whether the diarist is a smuggler or a pianist. Remember, the key term is *diaries* instead of *journals*.

--Blogs

Blogs serve today as a sort of public diary and illustrate the time or situation in a very personal way (e.g., *Birding Babylon: A soldier's journal from Iraq*). A search on **[your topic] and blogs** will not yet get numerous hits, but any blog that does make it to book form should be a very good read.

MAGIC SEARCH: [research interest or person] and (correspondence or diaries or personal narratives or blogs)

CHAPTER 9

FINDING PRIMARY SOURCES

--Sources
--Archives
Unparalleled for finding collections of documentary materials of all types: diaries, letters, speeches, and even memorabilia and photographs.

⊘ **RULE:** **--Archives** goes with people and organizations; **--Sources** goes with topics. Be safe with this:

🔍 **MAGIC SEARCH:** [research interest] and (sources or archives)

--Correspondence
For the personal correspondence of people, either as individuals or in groups: Amelia Earhart, say, or women air pilots (her "class of persons," according to the Library of Congress).
See also **--Records and correspondence**, used for the letters of organizations, industries, and institutions.

🔍 **MAGIC SEARCH:** [research interest] and correspondence

--Diaries
This term, used instead of *journals,* covers "registers or records of personal experiences, observations, thoughts, or feelings" (Library of Congress 2008a, H1538). The Library of Congress adds four conditions: **--Diaries** must be "kept daily or at frequent intervals," "written as an aid to memory or reflection," "intended for private rather than public use," and "contemporaneous with the events described" (Library of Congress 2008a, H1538).

--Personal narratives
Good news: eyewitness and autobiographical accounts only, no hearsay.

Bad news: For events and wars only, according to the Library of Congress.

Good news: The Library of Congress defines war generously: "armed conflicts called by other names, such as coups, revolutions, insurrections, uprising, invasions, or civil wars" (Library of Congress 2008a, H1200).

More good news: almost anything can be called an event: earthquakes, eruptions, terrorist attacks, and the Great Depression.

(!) **NOTE:** "Prior to 1977, the subdivision was used more widely under classes of persons, types of activities, and diseases. Those uses were replaced by the subdivision **--Biography** under classes of persons" (Library of Congress 2008a, H1928).

(◉) **RECOMMENDATION:** The scope of **--Personal narratives** should be returned to its expanded, pre-1977 state.

--Pamphlets

If the word *pamphlet* calls to mind those "Is it a migraine?" flyers you find in your doctor's office, think again! Pamphlets were the blogs of the day—in sixteenth- to eighteenth-century Europe and America, that is. More precisely, they were "short, separately published, usually polemical, essays or treatises regarding controversial issues of contemporary interest, especially political or religious matters" (Library of Congress 2008a, H1095).

(⊕) **BONUS FEATURE:** Libraries with resources like Early English Books Online or Evans's Early American Imprints will shine with **--Pamphlets.**

--Facsimiles

Use **--Facsimiles** to find "exact copies of [printed or written materials, documents, etc.], the originals of which were published or made at an earlier date" (Library of Congress 2008a, H1595). What might these be? Autographs; Mozart scores; and maps of Pocahontas County, West Virginia!

--Interviews

A great way to get the personal angle on a topic, **--Interviews** is also the subdivision of choice for invaluable oral histories.

See also **--Anecdotes**, in chapter 8, "Finding True Stories."

(🔍) **MAGIC SEARCH:** [research interest] and (interviews or personal narratives)
   Or strike the mother lode of primary sources with this:

(🔍) **MAGIC SEARCH:** [research interest] and (archives or sources or diaries or correspondence or narratives or interviews or facsimiles)

--Pictorial works

Add this subdivision to a search and limit the results instantly to works that are at least 50 percent pictures. Collections of photographs, sometimes the best contemporary record of an event, are described by **--Pictorial works**.
See also **--Portraits** under names of individual persons who lived after A.D. 1400, under individual families, and under classes of persons, ethnic groups, and individual wars.

--Photographs

Reserved for "photographic prints or digital photographs" themselves "rather than reproductions of photographs" (e.g., as collected in books) (Library of Congress 2008a, H1935). The result? Currently, **--Photographs** is most useful in special collections and archives that catalog their photographic holdings. As more libraries catalog their digital materials, searches on **--Photographs** are likely to increase in value.

--Caricatures and cartoons

Not a heavy hitter in terms of the quantity of results, but this subdivision is likely to produce a unique record of contemporary sentiment about a topic.

Campaign: A cartoon history of Bill Clinton's race for the White House

--Notebooks, sketchbooks, etc.

Esoteric? Esoteric and amazing! This subdivision pulls high numbers of results, most of which are largely primary material. The variety is rich and unpredictable. As an example, novelist Reynolds Price analyzes his emerging characters, explores story lines, and relates conversations with his editor in his book *Learning a trade: A craftsman's notebooks, 1955-1997.*

Striking in: The early notebooks of James Dickey

Thomas Jefferson's scrapbooks

--Maps

For cartographic atlases or individual maps. The researcher seeking old maps should add **--Early works to 1800** or **--Facsimiles** to the search.

CHAPTER 10

$$\bigotimes$$

IT'S ABOUT TIME

Time Periods and Chronological Subdivisions

The Library of Congress expresses time periods in many different ways—many, many, many, many different ways, and even with four *many*s it's an understatement! Lois Chan (2005, 102) explains the structure of chronological subdivisions: "The division into chronological periods varies according to place and to subject: scholarly consensus is the general guide."

As a result of these scholarly underpinnings, searchers will see digits, proper names, specialized vocabulary—1910-1936; To 332 B.C.; 18th century: Ming dynasty; Jurassic—not just lists of dates.

In practice, the very quality and depth of the Library of Congress's work make the use of chronological subdivisions challenging. **France--History** has nearly one hundred chronological subdivisions, and Great Britain uses nineteen just to get from 55 B.C. to A.D. 1300 (five periods, eleven kings, one family [the Plantagenets], one century, and one 621-year span)!

We'll tell you a little bit—quite a lot, really—about chronological subdivisions and then provide effective search tips. Note that "chronological subdivision" refers to the specific Library of Congress–created subdivision, while "time period" is any span of time a researcher may have in mind.

Let's start by using two place/subtopic situations to show how chronological subdivisions work.

SITUATION 1: SAME TIME PERIOD + SAME SUBTOPIC + DIFFERENT PLACES = DIFFERENT CHRONOLOGICAL SUBDIVISIONS

The time period is 1861–1865. The subtopic is history. For the United States, 1861–1865 has special meaning, the beginning and end of the Civil War. What was going on in the rest of the world during those years? Here are several countries with the same subtopic of history. Note the variety of chronological subdivisions that cover 1861–1865.

Kenya--History--To 1895

Uruguay--History--1830-1875

Canada--History--1841-1867

Vietnam--History--1858-1945

Australia--History--1788-1900

France--History--1848-1870

This major event in the United States might have had a ripple effect in other places, but that has no effect on those places' chronological subdivisions. So the keyword search **1861-1865 and Canada** is not likely to find results.

SITUATION 2: SAME TIME PERIOD + SAME PLACE + DIFFERENT SUBTOPICS = DIFFERENT CHRONOLOGICAL SUBDIVISIONS

Each subtopic related to one particular place has its own set of chronological subdivisions. The test question: What was going on in Great Britain in the Roaring Twenties? Here are some subject headings that would lead to answers:

Great Britain--Intellectual life--20th century

Great Britain--Foreign relations--1901-1936

Great Britain--Foreign relations--1910-1936 (yes, it's 1910!)

Great Britain--Social life and customs--20th century

Great Britain--Politics and government--1901-1936

Great Britain--Politics and government--1910-1936

Remember, library catalogs don't do math! They just match up characters. So a keyword search on **Great Britain and 1920s** or **Great Britain and twenties** would not pick up all the books that these subject headings describe.

As you might expect, the Library of Congress uses chronological subdivisions to analyze many topics. Here are a few examples.

Different types of music have their own sets of subdivisions. Chamber music starts with one nine-hundred-year span, **--500-1400**, then moves on with centuries, from **--15th century** through **--21st century**. Jazz, on the other hand, uses divisions by decade, starting with **--1910-1920** and ending, for now, at **--2001-2010**.

Do not assume, having seen these jazz subdivisions, that decade breakdowns apply elsewhere. Many topics have one-hundred-year breakdowns and nothing shorter. These, by the way, are presented as digits. It's **--18th century**, not eighteenth century.

Art topics usually receive the century treatment, with three exceptions: Chinese, Japanese, and Korean art. Each has its own set of chronological subdivisions, each of which is highly refined. For instance, Chinese art starts with **--To 221 B.C.**, proceeds through five dynasties that end with **--Ming-Qing, 1368-1912**, then finishes off with two century subdivisions: **--20th century** and **--21st century**.

And the first shall come last. Geologic time periods have their own vocabulary altogether: **--Jurassic, --Cambrian, --Mississippian**, and so on.

Tick, tick, tick . . . BOOM! There is no guessing the right keyword to use to express time. A search based on even an educated guess will bomb. The searcher must find out exactly which chronological subdivisions exist for the topic at hand.

THE SOLUTIONS: ONE PRACTICAL, ONE COMPLETE, ONE QUICK AND DIRTY

Start with a subject search. What? What about that freewheeling keyword search mode recommended throughout this book? Sorry, not this time.

The Practical Solution

The practical, and best, move is to do a subject search on the topic of interest, browse the list of results for chronological subdivisions, and choose the one that covers the time you're interested in.

The Complete Solution

Searchers who want to know all of the chronological possibilities, not just the ones that appear in their catalog, should use *Library of Congress Authorities.* This amazing work is available to everyone for free! At http://authorities .loc.gov, choose "Search Authorities," select "Subject Authority Headings," enter your topic, and behold the chronological subdivisions for any topic that merits them: English literature, existentialism, medicine.

The Quick and Dirty Solution

The bold soul can take a chance on the oft-present century subdivision with something like this:

🔍 **MAGIC SEARCH: [topic] and (18* or 19th) and not 18th.** "And not 18th" eliminates 1700–1799, leaving the searcher with the desired time period 1800–1899.

OTHER SUBDIVISIONS THAT EXPRESS TIME

--Chronology
Don't want to bother with specific dates or decades? Want the whole enchilada? Then **--Chronology** is the way to go! **[Topic] and chronology** will get a time line that places events in the order that they occurred.

--Longitudinal studies
Identifies "case studies in which variables related to a topic or group of people are assessed over a period of time or observed at successive stages in order to determine change or stability" (Library of Congress 2008a, H1848).

--Early works to . . .
A hint that the work has not been on the best-seller list lately. This phrase makes it clear that the work was written or published for the first time a long time ago. Usually the cutoff date is 1800, but some topics, such as electricity and psychiatry, use "a date other than 1800 . . . to bring out a date having more significance than 1800" (Library of Congress 2008a, H1576). The material can be reissued in the twenty-first century, but it will always be **--Early works to . . .**
Consider also

> **--Pre-Linnean works.** Anything written before 1735 on the topics of botany, zoology, or natural history. Search results are surprisingly numerous, given the esoteric sound of the subdivision.

> **--Early accounts to 1600.** Old, yes, but covers accounts of the Americas only.

--Forecasting
What will the future bring? "Predictions, conjectures, or calculations of future conditions, trends, or occurrences" (Library of Congress 2008a, H1628). Note the related **--Forecasts**, which the Library of Congress decided should describe one specific kind of prediction, those concerned with a century, with no particular subtopic specified. For instance, **Twenty-second century--Forecasts.** Frankly, we don't see the need.

> ⊚ **RECOMMENDATION:** The Library of Congress should drop **--Forecasting** and use **--Forecasts** for any work that predicts what lies ahead.

To borrow from Bob Dylan, the times they are a-changin' (and they try librarians' souls).

CHAPTER 11

TOOLS FOR SCHOLARS AND OTHER PROFESSIONALS

A thorough researcher will want to delve into a topic, and these subdivisions will help!

--Indexes

According to the Library of Congress's Cataloger's Desktop (2008a, H1670), indexes provide "comprehensive" coverage of a subject. The value is the thought involved in organizing the index. The results benefit any scholar who needs to find "everything" on a specific topic but must search with time-saving precision. The title *Index to the literature of American economic entomology* demonstrates just how specific these indexes can be!

***See also* --Concordances** in chapter 13, "Useful for the Humanities."

--Bibliography

For finding lists of books and articles; these lists are often annotated. If the subdivision is assigned to a person, the bibliography may be a list of the person's works or a list of works *about* the person. Because most bibliographies are selective, they can serve as guides to the literature on a topic.

⊘ **RULE:** If a bibliography is arranged by subject and is "comprehensive," and thus works as an index, the cataloger should assign **--Indexes** instead of **--Bibliography** (Library of Congress 2008a, H1670). What?

⊘ **RECOMMENDATION:** If the Library of Congress really believes that this rule is worth keeping, it should loosen up a bit and instruct catalogers to assign *both* subdivisions, **--Bibliography** and **--Indexes**.

--Historiography

Read about the study of a discipline or topic, including trends in scholarship and descriptions of the best—and worst—works in the field. Some historiographies, like *Peasants, class, and capitalism: The rural research of L. N. Kritsman and his school,* will serve serious scholars only—or librarians advising those scholars. Others, like *Extra innings: Writing on baseball,* surprise the aficionado by bringing to light titles he or she didn't know existed. As you can see from these two titles, **--Historiography** is not limited to history!

⊛ **MAGIC SEARCH:** [topic] and (bibliography or indexes or historiography)

--Chronology
Allows the scholar to examine the day-by-day accounts of any thing or any person.

> *The Civil War and Reconstruction: An eyewitness history*
> *Dates in oncology*
> *Wordsworth: The chronology of the early years, 1770-1799*

--Terminology
For the person looking for the best way to articulate something.

> *Perfect Phrases for Writing Grant Proposals*
> *Speleological and karst glossary of Florida and the Caribbean*

⊕ **BONUS FEATURE:** These often get at how to do something well by using the accepted terminology. Sound erudite in any field!

See also chapter 4, "Words, Words, . . . and Numbers," for information about **--Dictionaries, --Glossaries, --Nomenclature**, and other related subdivisions.

--Periodicals
Do you have a journal devoted to fungi? What periodicals do you have that discuss nineteenth-century literature? People can use this to browse the journal holdings of their own library.

--Book reviews
--Reviews

> **--Book reviews** allows the researcher to find a collection of book reviews on a topic. This can be useful for finding critiques of key books in a discipline. Librarians and professionals can use these as selection tools or for readers' advisory. **Sociology and book reviews** finds *Required reading: Sociology's most influential books.*

> **--Reviews** finds collections of reviews of any type of "artistic productions" or "performances" (Library of Congress 2008a, H2021). A scholar may learn about the viewer, and possibly the process of reviewing, as well as the production under review. The reviews themselves are of a higher quality than those done by, say, your average Amazon customer:

> *Writing in the dark, dancing in the New Yorker,* by Arlene Croce
> *Distinguishing features: film criticism and comment,* by Stanley Kauffman

⊛**MAGIC SEARCH:** [research interest] and reviews

--Standards
Provides an authoritative answer for how things should be done. The topics go far beyond science and technology; every area seems to have its set of standards (accounting, the environment, clock- and watchmaking).

--Methodology
--Research

> **--Methodology** explains "both the theory and practice of procedures to be followed" (Library of Congress 2008a, H1095). Find out how research in a discipline is done and how to conduct the research. This is not for amateurs (*Gray's dissection guide for human anatomy*).

> **--Research** does not find the results of research! Instead, it is about *how* to do research in any discipline. Often overlaps with **--Methodology.**

⊛**MAGIC SEARCH:** [topic] and (methodology or research)

--Laboratory manuals
--Fieldwork
If you need procedures and protocols for a "scientific" or "technical" topic in the laboratory, use **--Laboratory manuals.** If you need techniques for observation in the field, use **--Fieldwork** (Library of Congress 2008a, H1095).

--Statistical methods
Find out how to solve problems using statistics (Library of Congress 2008a, H1095). Titles won't necessarily have the statistics themselves, but they will explain how to use or collect them.

> *Basic biostatistics: Statistics for public health practice*
> *Reasoning with statistics: How to read quantitative research*

CHAPTER 12

SUBDIVISIONS THAT GIVE PERSPECTIVE, PUT YOU IN CONTROL, AND AMAZE OTHERS!

The subdivisions in this chapter truly perform magic in a library catalog and were the inspiration for the article that led to this book! They put spin, in its positive sense, on a topic and allow you to finesse a search. The first category below presents the "Aspects," which we fondly refer to as the Royal Family of Subdivisions. (You will see why we bow to them regularly.) The second category lists subdivisions that enable you to control the direction of a search (how A affects B, or how B affects A).

Use these subdivisions to impress your colleagues! Find results that make your patrons say, "How did you do that?"

THE ASPECTS, THE ROYAL FAMILY OF SUBDIVISIONS

Relationships Are Not Just for People!

The aspects subdivisions reveal the relationships between topics. The relationship is often based on how one topic affects the other, though the effect is not always direct or measurable. The "Aspects" also allow you to save a student from boring-topic-selection syndrome. Take an overused, generic, or way-too-broad topic and revitalize it by searching different facets. For example, test the topic **nuclear warfare** with the following subdivisions:

--**Psychological aspects** for how nuclear warfare affects "the mental condition or personality of individuals" (Library of Congress 2008a, H1095):

Children's fears of war

Heal or die: Psychotherapists confront nuclear annihilation

--**Social aspects** for how nuclear warfare affects society (and vice versa):

The Strangelove legacy: Children, parents and teachers in the nuclear age

The plutonium culture: From Hiroshima to Harrisburg

--**Health aspects** for how nuclear warfare affects a person's health:

> *The reluctant survivors: A family guide to the prevention and treatment of radiation sickness*

--**Environmental aspects** for how nuclear warfare affects our environment:

> *Nuclear winter: The evidence and the risks*
>
> *Planet Earth in jeopardy: Environmental consequences of nuclear war*

--**Economic aspects** for how nuclear warfare affects the economy:

> *Nuclear blast effects on a metropolitan economy*
>
> *Markets, distribution, and exchange after societal cataclysm: Final report*

What's Your Angle?

The aspects are also great for taking an angle on any given topic and are "especially good for unlikely pairings" (Kornegay, Buchanan, and Morgan 2005, 45).

--**Moral and ethical aspects** is attached to "non-religious or non-ethical topics" (e.g., chess, emotions, leadership, theater) (Library of Congress 2008a, H1095).

--**Political aspects** is paired with "non-political topics" (e.g., body image, dance, mass media, rugby football) (Library of Congress 2008a, H1095).

--**Physiological aspects** goes with "mental conditions" (loneliness, memory) and activities (golf, singing) (Library of Congress 2008a, H1095).

⊛ **MAGIC SEARCH: [topic] and aspects** will allow you to see all the interesting facets of a subject at once! Make a dull topic sparkle!

ⓘ **NOTE:** There are other aspects that are not quite such stellar performers (e.g., sociological aspects). We have listed our favorites, but any aspects will be swept up along with the others in the Magic Search.

SUBDIVISIONS THAT CONTROL

What Do You Think about That?

--**Attitudes**
--**Views on**

Both of these subdivisions tell how someone feels about something—their opinion on the topic. --**Attitudes** goes with groups of people; --**Views on** is for individuals. So women have --**Attitudes**; Edith Wharton has --**Views on**.

Cuban revolutionaries have **--Attitudes**; Fidel Castro has **--Views on**. Construction workers and teachers have **--Attitudes**. Machiavelli and Harry Truman have **--Views on**.

⊘**RULE:** Views on five areas—ethics, aesthetics, religion, society, and politics—have their very own subdivisions: **--Ethics**, **--Aesthetics**, **--Religion**, and **--Political and social views**. In our view, the **--Views on** pattern serves well, so we offer a recommendation:

⊘**RECOMMENDATION:** The Library of Congress should use **--Views on** for everything, including the preceding five areas.

--Public opinion
Presents the flip side of **--Attitudes** and **--Views on**, offering the "predominant attitude of a community of people on a topic" (Library of Congress 2008a, H1955). Nothing escapes the public's judging eye: plastic surgery, Martians, vegetarianism, adultery, bear hunting. People, too: Native Americans, Franz Liszt, serial killers. And let's be honest, how did people really feel about George Washington?

⊕ **BONUS FEATURE:** A good source of those ever-popular pro or con arguments.

See also **--Foreign public opinion**, used "to designate opinion about a region or country held by the residents of another region or country" (Library of Congress 2008a, H1955).

See also **--Appreciation**, used to describe public reception, praise, and the like of a person's artistic and literary works. Picasso, for example, could get both **--Appreciation** (for his body of work) and **--Public opinion** (for his love life, perhaps).

Did What, and to Whom?

--Influence
Examines the big picture, the long view. Note the singular, please! What lasting influence did George Orwell have? Starbucks Coffee Company? Surrealism? Judaism? The Bhagavad Gita? World War I? These examples represent the categories of topics that can have **--Influence**: individuals, corporate bodies, art forms and movements, religions, sacred works, and individual wars.

--Effect of [. . .] on
Addresses the more direct effect of one thing on another. Here plants, animals, materials, and parts of the body are major players. With a topic in mind—weeds, ears, paint, vehicles—it is simple to find results that show

how the topic is affected by something else. Weeds by drought, ears by vibration, paint by air pollution, and vehicles by explosive devices!

Is it Magic Search time? Perhaps **[research interest] and (influence or effect of)**? Afraid not. The list of **--Effect of [. . .] on** subdivisions goes on and on, and "effect of" and "influence" occur in numerous titles and contents notes. As a result, a keyword search for **[research interest] and effect of** or **[research interest] and influence** can quickly turn treacherous and hard to control. But should your catalog support keyword-in-subject searching, then the magic is back in a wink.

--[. . .] influences
Fill in the blank with anything from this long list: "civilizations of particular places larger than cities, . . . aspects of those civilizations, including art forms, literary forms, philosophies, intellectual life, . . . ethnic groups" (Library of Congress 2008a, H1675). Some examples: Zen influences, Jewish influences, Byzantine influences, African influences, and Western influences.

Consider also **--Foreign influences**, for "works discussing general outside cultural influences" (Library of Congress 2008a, H1675).

--Sources
It is said that inspiration can strike at any moment. How fortunate when the source that "served as the person's sources of ideas or inspiration" (Library of Congress 2008a, H1095) is documented—and even assigned its own subdivision. **James Joyce and sources** finds *Joyce and Dante: The shaping imagination;* **Keats and sources** leads to *Keats as a reader of Shakespeare;* and **Robert E. Lee and sources** reveals *Lee in the shadow of Washington.*

⊕ **BONUS FEATURE:** Books with **--Sources** usually have a second subject heading that identifies the inspirer in addition to the inspired. *Chaucer and Boccaccio* is about Boccaccio's shaping the work of Chaucer. The book has, therefore, two subject headings: Chaucer, with his **--Sources**, and Boccaccio, with his **--Influence**. Neat work, eh?

CHAPTER 13

USEFUL FOR THE HUMANITIES

FAVORITES FOR THE HUMANITIES

--Criticism and interpretation
--History and criticism
Your best bet for getting to criticism, evaluation, or explication, especially literary criticism. What, you may ask, is the difference between the two? It's all about what they may be attached to.

> **--Criticism and interpretation** is paired with an individual—any literary author, musician, or artist (Library of Congress 2008a, H1110).

> **--History and criticism** is attached to "literary, music, film, television program, and video recording" forms, such as Arabic poetry, German wit and humor, horror films, and salsa music (Library of Congress 2008a, H1095). Fine art (sigh) is not included.

⊘ **RECOMMENDATION:** There may have been a scholarly reason for not assigning **--History and criticism** to art topics, but we recommend that it be assigned to *all* artistic formats.

Consider also **--Criticism, Textual**, which is useful for examining or comparing specific "manuscripts and editions" (Library of Congress 2008a, H1110). This one is for serious literary scholars.

--Bio-bibliography
Identifies items, such as the wonderful *Dictionary of literary biography,* that contain biographical info in addition to bibliographies. Use **--Bio-bibliography** with topics, types of literature, ethnic groups, and places. This subdivision is assigned to resources that discuss "more than one person" (Library of Congress 2008a, H1328), which means that you are likely to find encyclopedic

resources that are arranged by topic, genre, or theme (e.g., Commonwealth, literature, blues music, medieval philosophy, Mexican artists).

This is perfect for the patron who says, "I'm supposed to do research on any Irish poet and I don't know where to start." Save the day by finding a list of Irish authors, accompanied by biographical information and bibliographies of major works by and about each author.

See also --**Bibliography**, the standby for lists of a person's works or works about a person or subject.

--Concordances

Locates "indexes to the principal words found within the writings of one author, one named work, or a group of literary works" (Library of Congress 2008a, H1670). --**Concordances** is also attached to sacred works, which makes it heaven sent for locating books that settle where-does-it-say-that-in-the-Bible? arguments.

> *A word index to Walden*
>
> *The analytical concordance to the New Revised Standard Version of the New Testament*
>
> *A concordance to F. Scott Fitzgerald's The Great Gatsby*

--Stories, plots, etc.

Leads to a wealth of information about the plots of literature, operas, musicals, ballets, and the like. Just the ticket to enrich an evening at the opera.

> *The Barefoot book of ballet stories*
>
> *Musical theater synopses*
>
> *Classics of science fiction and fantasy literature*

⊕ **BONUS FEATURE:** This subdivision will often find books about the performing arts that contain much more than just plot synopses, such as historical backgrounds, time and place of premieres, fascinating trivia, opera-night etiquette, and even advice on what to wear.

--Appreciation

Use this subdivision to understand the "public response and reception, praise, etc.," of an author, artist, musician, or topic (Library of Congress 2008a, H1110).

> *Soldier's heart: Reading literature through peace and war at West Point*
>
> *1001 paintings you must see before you die*
>
> *Beethoven in German politics, 1870-1989*
>
> *Worshipping Walt: The Whitman disciples*

--Influence

Use this to read about the influence of an individual, a group of people, a religion, or a movement (Library of Congress 2008a, H1110).

> *American Chaucers*
>
> *The Africanist aesthetic in global hip-hop: Power moves*
>
> *The impact of the Holocaust on Jewish theology*

If you want to understand a person's stature (how she or he was appreciated and the influence that person had), try this:

🔍 **MAGIC SEARCH: [person] and (appreciation or influence)**

--Chronology

For finding dates and important events that provide historical context. Important figures in the humanities often have multivolume sets that detail their lives and artistic works.

--Homes and haunts

Points out books about individuals and their surroundings: Monet's gardens, Robert Frost living in England, Harriet Beecher Stowe in Florida, American women authors in Italy. Results are exceptionally unpredictable and unfailingly interesting.

--Themes, motives

According to Merriam-Webster Online, a motive, or motif, is "a usually recurring salient thematic element (as in the arts); *especially:* a dominant idea or central theme." Find themes and motifs addressed by artists such as Fyodor Dostoyevsky, Bob Marley, or Frank Lloyd Wright. Also, learn how themes or motifs are used in certain "literary and art forms" (e.g., modern art, Welsh literature, sepulchral monuments!) (Library of Congress 2008a, H1095).

➕ **BONUS FEATURE:** Often reveals reference books that allow you to search by a certain theme or motif:

> *The tattoo encyclopedia: A guide to choosing your tattoo*
>
> *Graphic novels: A genre guide to comic books, manga, and more*
>
> *The storyteller's sourcebook: A subject, title, and motif index to folklore collections for children*

--Notebooks, sketchbooks, etc.

Allows you to follow (or read about) the creative process of artists, writers, musicians, philosophers, and the like.

> *Descartes' secret notebook*
>
> *Thomas Hardy's "Facts" notebook*
>
> *A Degas sketchbook*

> *Artaria 195: Beethoven's sketchbook for the Missa solemnis and the*
> *Piano sonata in E major, opus 109*

--Facsimiles

For viewing exact copies "of printed or written materials, documents, etc., . . . the originals of which were published or made at an earlier date" (Library of Congress 2008a, H1595). For most of us, this will be as close as we get to important manuscripts and documents outside of a rare books room or archive.

--Manuscripts

Want to read about manuscripts? Intimidating rules abound, but generally **--Manuscripts** is "used under topical headings for works that discuss collections of manuscripts on those topics" (Library of Congress 2008a, H1855) and under individuals "for works discussing writings made by hand, typewriter, etc., by or about the person" (Library of Congress 2008a, H1110).

> *The early medieval Bible: Its production, decoration, and use*
>
> *The compositional process of J. S. Bach: A study of the autograph scores of the vocal works*
>
> *The literary manuscripts of Henry David Thoreau*

(!) **NOTE:** The Library of Congress gives us many subdivisions, such as **--Photographs**, that identify a specific form, but when it comes to original manuscripts, the subdivision **--Manuscripts** applies only to works *about* manuscripts. For original manuscripts, the Library of Congress instructs catalogers to assign the main heading Manuscripts (Library of Congress 2008a, H1855).

See also **--Early works to 1800** and **--Archives** and **--Notebooks, sketchbooks, etc.** and chapter 9, "Finding Primary Sources."

ART

--Catalogues raisonnés

Interested in a comprehensive list of an artist's works, just looking for one medium or all media, would you like it chronologically or systematically, and would you like descriptive or critical notes with that? **--Catalogues raisonnés** delivers all of this!

> *Bruegel: The complete paintings, drawings and prints*
>
> *James McNeill Whistler: Drawings, pastels, and watercolours:*
> *A catalogue raisonné*

--Art collections

Combine in a keyword search with a favorite artist to find images you may not see anywhere else. Or look for a collector (a Medici or a queen, perhaps).

--In art

Find out how any place, organization, or Christian denomination is portrayed in artwork.

ⓘ **NOTE:** A keyword search also finds instances where topics are paired with "in art" to form main subject headings like Unicorns in art or Food in art.

--Design and construction
--Design

> **--Design and construction** unveils how something (e.g., a Gothic cathedral, a skyscraper) was constructed or how to construct something (e.g., mosques, stage props).

> **--Design** finds titles that explain how to design or that talk about the design of things that, according to Library of Congress (2008a, H1532) are not constructed (e.g., gardens, knit goods).

Because not even catalogers are clear on whether things like shoes can be constructed, or are instead merely designed, try this:

✪ **MAGIC SEARCH: [object] and design**

See also **--Designs and plans**, perfect for the architect or interior designer.

Other useful subdivisions for art

--Attribution
--Conservation and restoration
--Copying
--Expertising
--Forgeries
--Reproduction

LANGUAGE

Studying Language

--Dialects

> *Tauk frum the hills*
> *American voices: How dialects differ from coast to coast*

Colloquial Arabic

The folk speech of East Yorkshire

--Etymology

Inventing English: A portable history of the language

The life of language: The fascinating ways words are born, live and die

--Grammar

Sister Bernadette's barking dog: The quirky history and lost art of diagramming sentences

--Inflection

A distributional approach to Yiddish inflection

Linguistic complexity: The influence of social change on verbal inflection

--Phonology

The sounds of Spanish

Tonality in Austronesian languages

Learning a Foreign Language

--Conversation and phrase books

General books for beginners and globe-trotters, as well as specialized phrase books for different professions (e.g., dental personnel, gourmets, soldiers).

Medical Spanish for health care professionals

An introduction to spoken Bolivian Quechua

Italian travel pack

--Composition and exercises

Perfect for teachers who need concrete strategies for teaching reading and writing. Also great for writers who want to improve their skills.

Powerful writing strategies for all students

Writing across distances and disciplines

Developing higher-level literacy in all students

--Textbooks for foreign speakers

English vocabulary for beginning ESL learners

Spanish demystified

Mandarin Chinese the easy way

Using Your Words Correctly
--Pronunciation

> *Say it in French*
>
> *Speaking to be understood: English as a first or second language*

--Errors of usage

> *Barron's 1001 pitfalls in English grammar*
>
> *Death sentences: How clichés, weasel words, and management-speak are strangling public language*
>
> *Problèmes de langage*

--Usage

> *English grammar for the utterly confused*

--Style
Use for locating excellent writing manuals like Strunk and White's classic and others:

> *The elements of style / by William Strunk Jr. and E. B. White*
>
> *The ABC of style; a guide to plain English*
>
> *College writing skills: A text with exercises*
>
> *Ambiguity in Greek literature; studies in theory and practice*

Ⓘ **NOTE:** Writers using "style" in their keyword searches will also pick up the subdivision **--Style manuals**.

LITERATURE

Below is a list of the most interesting subdivisions for literature. Those literary scholars who want to find everything about an author should do a subject search on the author's name, and then browse the list of subdivisions that unfolds.

--Authorship
--Technique
--Literary style
This trio covers the process of an author's writing.

> **--Authorship.** The Library of Congress assigns **--Authorship** to "disciplines, and under literary, motion picture, radio, television, and video forms and genres" (Library of Congress 2008a, H1095). A search for **authorship and horror** will unveil works that show the how-to aspects of authorship

(*Create-a-monster: Writing a horror story*), give biographical information about authors writing in a certain genre (*R. L. Stine: Creator of creepy and spooky stories*), or interview authors (or just one author) about their writing (*Speaking of horror: Interviews with writers of the supernatural*). **--Authorship** is also attached to individuals for "discussions on the attribution of authorship of works to the person" (Library of Congress 2008a, H1110).

--Technique. Expresses the details "of individual literary authors and . . . literary form headings for works on writing technique" (Library of Congress 2008a, H1095).

--Literary style. Use for researching a literary author's "discussions of rhetoric, figures of speech, and artistic use of language in general" (Library of Congress 2008a, H1110).

Holy subdivisions, Batman! It is often hard to figure out why **--Literary style** has been assigned rather than **--Technique** (or vice versa). To further confuse matters, resources that cover the writing style or technique of authors in different genres can be assigned **--Authorship**. Exploit this abundance of subdivisions with the following:

🔍**MAGIC SEARCH:** [your author or genre] and (technique or style or authorship)

--Characters
Examines characters portrayed in an author's work.

> *The wisdom of Harry Potter*
> *George Eliot and her heroines: A study*
> *Importing Madame Bovary: The politics of adultery*

--Folklore
--Legends

--Folklore. Identifies collections of folktales about any topic (e.g., cockroaches), a place (e.g., Senegal), or any group of people (e.g., magicians). Great for the researcher who wants a new version of a classic tale.

--Legends. Covered by the folklore umbrella, this subdivision is assigned in particular to "literary versions of legendary tales about" a person, character, sacred work, or religious topic (Library of Congress 2008a, H1095). The Library of Congress identifies legends as those "which have come down from the past and which are popularly taken as historical though not verifiable" (Library of Congress 2008a, H1110).

> *The frontiersman: The real life and the many legends of Davy Crockett*
> *The Middle English miracles of the Virgin*

⊛**MAGIC SEARCH:** [research interest] and (legends or folklore)

--Mythology
Pinpoints discussions of how the human body, plants, horses, and so on, are portrayed in mythology.

--Romances
Finds the texts of romances. Perhaps not what first comes to mind as romance, this subdivision refers to the true literary definition of romance: a medieval European tale (Library of Congress 2008a, H1095). If you are looking for bodice rippers or the romanticism of Samuel Taylor Coleridge and William Wordsworth, you will be disappointed.

READERS' ADVISORY

--Stories, plots, etc.
The key to finding readers' advisory guides, this subdivision highlights resources that give plot summaries; many of these resources allow you to browse by plot.

The romance readers' advisory: The librarian's guide to love in the stacks

The book club companion

Genreflecting: A guide to reading interests in genre fiction

Laura's list: The first lady's list of 57 great books for families and children

See also **--Themes, motives**.

--Books and reading
Allows you to raid the reading lists of famous people or get recommendations for any reader.

Thoreau's reading

"Well acquainted with books": The founding framers of 1787

The mother-daughter book club

--Literary collections
Finds anthologies that contain a mix of formats (e.g., poetry, plays, short stories). These collections are great reads on their own, or use them to guide you to new authors who write about your interests.

--Bibliography
A discovery tool that provides lists of reads by or about your favorite author or about any reading interest.

MUSIC AND THE PERFORMING ARTS

Music

--Songs and music
Finds printed or recorded music about any topic.

> *Kennedy's blues: African-American blues and gospel songs on JFK*
>
> *People take warning! Murder ballads and disaster songs, 1913-1938* (sound recording)
>
> *Music of the Miskito Indians of Honduras and Nicaragua* (sound recording)
>
> *Suffragist sheet music*

--Musical settings
"Writings or words" of an individual, "set to music" (Library of Congress 2008a, H1110).

> *Little Women: An opera in two acts*

--Scores
A word about scores! It is best to use **--Scores** with an additional music term for manageable results, such as *vocal, piano, chorus, symphonies, parts, excerpts, arranged,* and so on.

About Music

--Analysis, appreciation

> *Poetry into song: Performance and analysis of lieder*
>
> *Unlocking the groove: Rhythm, meter, and musical design in electronic dance music*
>
> *Miles Davis, Miles smiles, and the invention of post bop*

--Interpretation (Phrasing, dynamics, etc.)
This can be viewed as the **--Handbooks, manuals, etc.** for musicians; great for professionals and amateurs who want to improve their musical skills.

--Methods
--Studies and exercises
--Instruction and study

🔍 **MAGIC SEARCH: [instrument] and (methods or exercises or instruction)** will get the how-to for teaching music or learning to play. The rest is practice, practice, practice! For even more practice, use **--Teaching pieces.**

Theater

--Dramatic production
--Stage history

These two are for plays only—no opera, no matter how dramatic it is, and no dance, even though dance usually involves a stage! --Dramatic production covers "various aspects of stage presentation, for example, acting, costume, stage setting and scenery" (Library of Congress 2008a, H1110). --Stage history does the same, but adds the historical angle. Fans of theater will want to do the following:

⊗ MAGIC SEARCH: [play or playwright] and (dramatic production or stage history)

All Performing Arts

--Production and direction

Highlights the how-to side of the performing arts, both the technical and business ends. The scope is wide: dance, erotic films, musicals, movies, opera, radio, television, and digital video editing.

The making of Miss Saigon
Fight choreography: The art of non-verbal dialogue
The business of TV production
Producing and the theatre business: Working in the theatre

--Stage-setting and scenery

Addresses the technical side of productions of all kinds: dance, theater, rock concerts, television shows.

Design for performance: From Diaghilev to the Pet Shop Boys
Stage rigging handbook
Technical theatre: A practical introduction

--Performances

For works about performances by individual artists—singers, actors, dancers, mezzo-sopranos—as well as performances of types of material, such as opera, rock music, and radio comedy.

⊕ BONUS FEATURE: --Performances also shines a light on composers and choreographers performing their own compositions and pieces.

Sarah Bernhardt's first American theatrical tour
The Callas legacy
Martha Graham in performance
Fats Waller on the air

--Reviews
Identifies collections of reviews of performances or "artistic productions," including music, dance, theater, and motion pictures (Library of Congress 2008a, H2021). These pieces are some of the best writing in the business.

--Pronunciation by foreign speakers
The surprising feature of this subdivision is its potential use for performers studying a role.

> *Foreign dialects: A manual for actors, directors and writers*
>
> *Scenes in dialect for young actors*
>
> *Singing in Czech*
>
> *Accents: A manual for actors*

--Drama
Identifies a play; a collection of plays; or a dramatic production on any topic, place, person, or group of people (Library of Congress 2008a, H1780).

Other useful subdivisions for music and the performing arts
--First performances
--Discography
--Librettos
--Filmography

RELIGION

--Essence, genius, nature
This "Who knew?" subdivision is perfect for curious people just starting their research. Pair this with a major religion and find introductions, backgrounds, and explanations.

> *What everyone needs to know about Islam*
>
> *What Buddhism is*
>
> *The structure of religion: Judaism and Christianity*

--Religion
Describes "general works on the religions or religious history" of places, ethnic groups, institutions, and individuals (Library of Congress 2008a, H1997). A keyword search will bring a flood of results, so be sure to add more specific terms to your search.

--Religious aspects
Performs like other "aspects" subdivisions, in this case getting at the religious angle of any nonreligious topic (e.g., earthquakes, human cloning, food, sports, water).

--Religious life
--Religious life and customs
These two deal with the day-to-day and personal aspects of religion.

> **--Religious life** finds "general works that describe personal religious and devotional life, or offer practical advice on developing behavior based on religious precepts" (Library of Congress 2008a, H2015.5).

> > *The women in God's kitchen: Cooking, eating, and spiritual writing*
> > *Forbidden fruit: Sex and religion in the lives of American teenagers*
> > *Mystics, mavericks, and merrymakers: An intimate journey among Hasidic girls*
> > *365 meditations for grandmothers by grandmothers*

Consider also **--Prayers and devotions** for advice-related materials.

> **--Religious life and customs** is "for works on the religious customs, practices, etc." of countries and cities (Library of Congress 2008a, H2016).

> > *Holy hills of the Ozarks: Religion and tourism in Branson*
> > *Ritual practice in modern Japan*
> > *Cultures of devotion: Folk saints of Spanish America*

🔍 **MAGIC SEARCH:** [research interest] and (religious aspects or religious life)

Other useful subdivisions for religion

--Customs and practices
Enlighten yourself with resources detailing the goings-on of different religions, monastic orders, and denominations.

> *The white nights of Ramadan*
> *What you will see inside a synagogue*
> *Buddhist festivals throughout the year*

--Comparative studies
Assigned to religious topics (e.g., creation, future life), sacred works, and denominations (Library of Congress 2008a, H1095).

> *The voice, the word, the books: The sacred scripture of the Jews, Christians, and Muslims*

--Controversial literature

Finds works, or descriptions of those works, that "express opposition toward" a certain religion, denomination, or sacred work (Library of Congress 2008a, H1472).

> *The God who wasn't there*
> *Killing the Buddha: A heretic's Bible*
> *The trouble with Islam*

--Apologetic works
--Catechisms
--Clergy
--Concordances
--Creeds
--Liturgical objects
--Liturgy
--Doctrines
--Missions
--Prayers and devotions
--Prophecies
--Rituals
--Sermons
--Theology
--Versions

CHAPTER 14

USEFUL FOR THE SOCIAL SCIENCES

BEST ALL-AROUND

--Case studies
Unearth a gold mine of real-life examples for just about any topic. Perfect for any social scientist and almost always fascinating reading.

Hello, Charlie: Letters from a serial killer

Love in the second act: True stories of romance, midlife and beyond

Reviving Ophelia: Saving the selves of adolescent girls

The presidential character: Predicting performance in the White House

Or, for the long-view version of case studies, use **--Longitudinal studies**, which produces research gems for social scientists.

Risk and resilience: Adolescent mothers and their children grow up

How college affects students: A third decade of research

--Social life and customs

This is the go-to subdivision for anthropologists, sociologists, and anyone else studying a country or group of people. Ideal for questions like, What is life like in Yemen? What do they do for fun in Finland? and What is an ordinary day like for aboriginal Australians?

Eating, drinking, and visiting in the South

Everyday life in Central Asia: Past and present

Teenage wasteland: Suburbia's dead end kids

--Psychological aspects

How can love, video games, dance, food, or the color blue affect a person's mental well-being? Use **--Psychological aspects** to analyze the influence of everyday things on "the mental condition or personality of individuals"

(Library of Congress 2008a, H1095). This overachiever will produce a multitude of results, from self-help titles (*Why him? why her? Finding true love by understanding your personality type*) to scholarly works (*Handbook of bereavement research and practice*).

--Psychology
It won't empower you to read minds, but **--Psychology** is great for examining the "psychological traits, personality, character, etc." of individuals (e.g., Fidel Castro) and groups of people (e.g., Mohave Indians, pet owners) (Library of Congress 2008a, H1095).

--Sex differences
Is the battle of the sexes still raging? Are men and women really from different planets? Find out by pairing **--Sex differences** with a topic, language, or—um—body part.

> *Sex and the brain: A reader*
>
> *The myth of Mars and Venus*
>
> *Why men never remember and women never forget*

--Age factors
> *Everyday cognition in adulthood and late life*
>
> *Intellectual development in adulthood*

--Cross-cultural studies
Explore how body language, food habits, social policy, and so on, differ between "two or more cultures or societies" (Library of Congress 2008a, H1510).

> *Families in a global context*
>
> *Intimacies: Love and sex across cultures*
>
> *A beautiful game: International perspectives on women's football*

--Public opinion
--Attitudes
> **--Public opinion** tells you what the general public thinks about a certain issue (e.g., deviant behavior, firearms, Social Security) or group (e.g., Choctaw Indians, teachers). Many catalog records will also specify where that public is located (e.g., Africa, Bangladesh, North Carolina).
>
> **--Attitudes** refers to what a specific group (e.g., children of divorced parents, homeowners, social workers, victims of crimes) thinks about anything.

--Economic aspects
--Economic conditions
Both subdivisions explore the economic situation. **--Economic aspects** is attached to topics (e.g., child care, drug abuse, free trade, gambling, intellectual property, mafia, nationalism, racism, zoning, and on and on), while **--Economic conditions** goes with places and groups of people. Can't remember which is which? Never fear, just remember that "economic" is singular, and economize with this:

⭐**MAGIC SEARCH:** [research interest] and (economic conditions or economic aspects)

PSYCHOLOGY

--Mental health
Reveals the "mental health or mental illness" of a specific group or individual and includes "accounts of specific disorders" (Library of Congress 2008a, H1890).

> *The aftermath: Living with the Holocaust*
> *When the bubble bursts: Clinical perspectives on midlife issues*

--Mental health services
Locates items "discussing organized services providing mental health care to [a] group" (Library of Congress 2008a, H1890).

⊕ **BONUS FEATURE:** Many titles offer practical advice for counselors, psychologists, and other mental health professionals.

> *Treating adult and juvenile offenders with special needs*
> *Special populations in college counseling: A handbook for mental health professionals*

Want to know everything about the personality, psychological characteristics, *and* mental health of an individual or group?

⭐**MAGIC SEARCH:** [person or group] and (mental health or psychology)

THE POLITICAL SUBDIVISIONS

--Politics and government
The leader in the world of political science subdivisions, **--Politics and government** will guide you to "the history of political events [of a place] and/or the history, description, or critical analysis of governmental and political

institutions, parties, organizations, etc." as well as to an ethnic group's "self-government" (Library of Congress 2008a, H1942).

> *The Pol Pot regime: Race, power, and genocide in Cambodia under the Khmer Rouge, 1975-79*
>
> *Leftovers: Tales of the Latin American left*
>
> *Dreams and shadows: The future of the Middle East*

--Political activity

Find out how individuals and groups (e.g., Baptists, celebrities, economists, labor unions, Muslims) participate in politics.

(!) **NOTE:** Use **--Political and social views** for individuals on their "general" views on politics and social issues (Library of Congress 2008a, H1110).

--Citizen participation

In addition to **--Political activity**, the Library of Congress gives us this one "for works on the participation of citizens in carrying out an activity" (Library of Congress 2008a, H1095). This time it is the activity upon which the Library of Congress places emphasis.

⊕ **BONUS FEATURE:** Find titles like *Citizen lobbyists: Local efforts to influence public policy.* Also, **--Citizen participation** includes resources that can tell you how to be a good citizen (*50 ways to save the earth*).

To find a range of resources on any kind of political participation or activism, try this:

🔍 **MAGIC SEARCH:** [activity/person/group] and (political activity or citizen participation)

--Political aspects

The "political dimensions or implications of nonpolitical topics" (Library of Congress 2008a, H1095). In an age where everything seems to be political, what is a nonpolitical topic? Try calypso music!

> *The political calypso: True opposition in Trinidad and Tobago, 1962-1987*
>
> *Beaches, ruins, resorts: The politics of tourism in the Arab world*
>
> *The political economy of college sports*

--Foreign relations
--Relations

> **--Foreign relations.** Describes official "diplomatic relations between . . . countries [or regions] and other sovereign states" (Library of Congress 2008a, H1629).

The next great clash: China and Russia vs. the United States

Nuclear matters in North Korea: Building a multilateral response for future stability in Northeast

The newer Caribbean: Decolonization, democracy, and development

--Relations. Now that you know the diplomatic stance, how are the places really getting along? **--Relations** reports the nondiplomatic relationships between specific places.

Cuba in the American imagination

The Soviet impact in Africa

Ⓘ **NOTE:** If the number of related places is three or more, the subdivision becomes **--Relations--Foreign countries**, with no mention of the specific places (Library of Congress 2008a).

Want both diplomatic and nondiplomatic relations?

🔍 **MAGIC SEARCH: [places] and relations**

If the results are too numerous or irrelevant, switch to the more conservative keyword-in-subject search.

--Foreign countries

This subdivision tells about natives of one country living in other countries. Imagine the word *in* added, as in "in foreign countries," and it will make more sense.

Emigrant nation: The making of Italy abroad (Italians in foreign countries)

Cuba: Idea of a nation displaced (Cubans in foreign countries)

THE SOCIAL SUBDIVISIONS

--Social aspects
--Social conditions
--Sociological aspects

No, they don't throw a lot of parties, but these subdivisions *do* get to the heart of social issues. **--Social aspects** is paired with things, **--Social conditions** with places and groups of people, and **--Sociological aspects** with institutions.

--Social aspects. Points you to the "effect of [an] item, activity, discipline, etc., and society on each other" (Library of Congress 2008a, H1095).

Drink: A cultural history of alcohol

The cult of thinness

The veil: Women writers on its history, lore, and politics

--Social conditions. "For works discussing the social history or sociology of a place, ethnic group, or class of persons" (Library of Congress 2008a, H2055).

> *Trapped in poverty: Chronic poor in remote tribal areas*
> *There's no José here: Following the hidden lives of Mexican immigrants*

--Sociological aspects. Used, according to the Cataloger's Desktop (Library of Congress 2008a, H1095), with "types of institutions for works discussing the impact of the inherent nature of the institution." The interpretation of exactly what qualifies as an institution varies widely. For instance, in some books, marriage is treated as an institution, and thus **--Sociological aspects** is applied. But sometimes marriage is just a plain old subject; thus, **--Social aspects** applies.

Want to just search and get on with your life?

🔍 **MAGIC SEARCH:** [research interest] and (Social or sociological) and (aspects or conditions)

LAW

--Law and legislation
--Legal status, laws, etc.
Get briefed on law topics with these two subdivisions. Both are great for people who are intimidated by the legalese used in statutes and codes (Kornegay, Buchanan, and Morgan 2005).

> **--Law and legislation.** Discloses the legal spin on every imaginable topic.

> > *On same-sex marriage, civil unions, and the rule of law*
> > *Make any divorce better! Specific steps to make things smoother, faster, less painful and save you a lot of money*
> > *Computer and Internet use on campus: A legal guide to issues of intellectual property, free speech, and privacy*

> **--Legal status, laws, etc.** Investigates legal issues related to people.

> > *Rights of the disabled*
> > *Indian feminisms: Law, patriarchies and violence in India*
> > *Dealing with problem employees: A legal guide*

ⓘ **NOTE:** If you are devotee of subdivisions such as **--Psychological aspects** or **--Social conditions**, you might expect that when it comes to law topics, the Library of Congress would have created "Legal aspects" for topics and "Legal conditions" for people. But instead the Library of Congress chose

--**Law and legislation** and --**Legal status, laws, etc.**, respectively. Your first response might be "I object!" but we are overruled and must trust the judgment of the Library of Congress.

--Cases
Searching for court cases on a specific issue can be challenging. Fortunately, --**Cases** applies to any legal topic and will bring us to compilations of cases relevant to a theme or subject area.

> *I dissent: Great opposing opinions in landmark Supreme Court cases*
>
> *Ethics and criminal justice: An introduction*
>
> *Equal play: Title IX and social change*

--Legal research
A boon for all legal researchers, law students, and librarians, this how-to subdivision brings materials that will help us successfully use resources like "court reports, codes, digests, citators, etc., in determining the status of statutory, regulatory, or case law on a topic" (Library of Congress 2008a, H1710).

> *The legal research dictionary: From advance sheets to pocket parts*
>
> *Legal information: What it is and where to find it*

--Trials, litigation, etc.
Bite into the juicy details of trials and related proceedings. --**Trials, litigation, etc.** is applied to "individual persons, families, corporate bodies, or jurisdictions for the proceedings of civil or criminal actions to which they are parties, or for works about such proceedings" (Library of Congress 2008a, H2228).

> *Bush v. Gore*
>
> *The state vs. Nelson Mandela*
>
> *The Microsoft case*

--Corrupt practices
Want to chase down an organization (e.g., Enron) or industry (e.g., meat industry) or activity (e.g., elections) in need of legal defense? Try --**Corrupt practices**!

> *The dark side of the diamond: Gambling, violence, drugs and alcoholism in the national pastime*
>
> *Deadly deception: General Electric, nuclear weapons and our environment*
>
> *A review of the evils that have prevailed in the linen manufacture of Ireland* (from 1762!)

--Moral and ethical aspects
Applicable to any research topic. It's legal, but is it ethical?

>*Moral constraints on war: Principles and cases*
>
>*Protecting participants and facilitating social and behavioral sciences research*

TESTS AND MEASURES

Because of protocols controlling the administration of tests, copies of actual tests can be difficult to obtain through a library, but these subdivisions do lead you to general information, methodology, and test results.

--Testing
"For works on the construction, application, and results of testing pertaining to . . . topics" (e.g., aggressiveness, memory, vocational interests) (Library of Congress 2008a, H1095).

--Ability testing
"For works on tests and testing of native aptitude or acquired proficiency in a particular topic" (e.g., bowling, critical thinking, reading) (Library of Congress 2008a, H2186).

--Psychological testing
Locates "works on methods and results of conducting psychological tests of" groups of people (e.g., employees, prisoners, teenagers) (Library of Congress 2008a, H2186).

--Intelligence testing
"For works on methods and results of conducting intelligence tests" on groups of people (Library of Congress 2008a, H2186). Children appear most commonly in search results, which is not surprising. When was the last time you took an intelligence test? If you saw this Magic Search coming, give yourself a score of 100.

🔍 **MAGIC SEARCH: [group or topic] and testing**

--Methodology
The perfect how-to for any social scientist, this hard worker is matched with "disciplines and other topical headings for works on both the theory and practice of procedures to be followed" (Library of Congress 2008a, H1095).

>*Political science research methods*
>
>*Analyzing social settings: A guide to qualitative observation and analysis*

Clinical anthropology: An application of anthropological concepts within clinical settings

--Statistical methods

For "discussions of the methods of solving problems . . . through the use of statistics" (Library of Congress 2007, SD-87). Find sources for your specific subject area or research interest.

Handbook of statistical modeling for the social and behavioral sciences

Sampling of populations: Methods and applications

How to collect and analyze data: A manual for sheriffs and jail administrators

--Statistics

Your best bet for finding "statistical data" or "works discussing statistical data" about topics (e.g., crime, early childhood), places (e.g., Chicago, France), and groups (e.g., gangs, referees) (Library of Congress 2008a, H2095).

Hispanic Americans: A statistical sourcebook

Cities ranked and rated: More than 400 metropolitan areas evaluated in the U.S. and Canada

National estimates of marriage dissolution and survivorship

Consider also --Statistical services for finding "general works describing services that collect numerical data" for different topics (but only if you are into that sort of thing) (Library of Congress 2008a, H2095).

CHAPTER 15

USEFUL FOR HISTORICAL RESEARCH

BEST ALL-AROUND

--History
--Civilization
The supreme rulers of historical research. The Library of Congress distinguishes between the two: "History is the chronological account of specific events, emphasizing political, diplomatic, military, and economic developments" (Library of Congress 2008a, H1370). Civilization "places particular emphasis on cultural advances, including the arts, learning and scholarship, intellectual life, manners and customs, the development and growth of religion, advances in science and technology, etc." (Library of Congress 2008a, H1370).

> **--History**. "History" could almost be a stop word in library catalogs, but that wouldn't do, no matter how many thousands of hits it brings, for **--History** is the preeminent subdivision for the historical treatment of any place or topic. If your catalog allows the powerful keyword-in-subject search, **--History** will be a winner for you. If not, best to browse for it in lists of subject results.

> **--Civilization**. For "works on the history of civilization of a particular place" (Library of Congress 2008a, H1370), so is it narrower than **--History**? Perhaps not, for this reason: works are assigned either **--History** or **--Civilization**, not both. Consider adding the century of interest in the form "18th century" (not "eighteenth century").

ⓘ NOTE: A keyword search will also get many useful subject headings of the form **[topic] and civilization**: War and civilization, Technology and civilization, and so on.

--Sources
--Archives
If you had to choose two subdivisions for finding primary sources, these would be the ones! Both describe collections of primary documents such as letters, speeches, household records, diaries.
See "Tools for Historians" later in this chapter for more details.

--Chronology
Gives a historical twist to any topic. Also excellent for a quick overview of a topic, as most book-length chronologies add text to time lines and lists of dates.

> *Into the air: An illustrated timeline of flight*
> *The arts in Ireland, a chronology*
> *This day in American history*

LIFE AND LIVES

--Social life and customs
For "works on the customs, ways of living, and habits of people and places" (Library of Congress 2008a, H2057). Essential for the student who asks, "What did people eat for breakfast in ancient Greece?"

--Social conditions
For "works discussing the social history or sociology" of a place or group of people (Library of Congress 2008a, H2055). Covers social problems, change, social institutions, and the like.

--Economic conditions
"For works discussing the economic history or economic conditions in general" of a place or group of people (Library of Congress 2008a, H1578).

--Contemporaries
--Adversaries
--Friends and associates
--Family
In order from the top: lived at the same time as the person, lived at the same time and opposed the person, knew the person well (or very well), and was related to the person.
Consider also --Court and courtiers. Kings and rulers are allowed --Paramours as well. Library of Congress keeps its rule for --Paramours well under cover, but it appears from searches that presidents, too, may have paramours.

--Captivity
--Imprisonment
--**Captivity** covers time as a hostage, under house arrest, and other miscellaneous times of confinement or bondage. Once the person enters a correctional facility or prisoner-of-war camp, --**Imprisonment** takes effect. If you're more interested in the lack of freedom than the particulars, try this:

⊛ **MAGIC SEARCH:** [person or group of people] and (imprisonment or captivity)

Consider also --**Exile**, --**Kidnapping**, --**Assassination**, and --**Assassination attempt**.

ⓘ **NOTE:** For people held by their own country as a national security risk, such as Japanese Americans during World War II, use --**Evacuation and relocation**.

PLACES

--Description and travel
The subdivision most commonly assigned to places. Includes general descriptive works and "accounts of travel" and the "history of travel" in a place (Library of Congress 2008a, H1530).

--Discovery and exploration
"For works on geographical exploration of places that are unsettled or sparsely settled and are unknown to the rest of the world" (Library of Congress 2008a, H1564).

--Early accounts to 1600
The good news: first-person accounts; the bad news: covers only the Americas.

⊛ **MAGIC SEARCH:** [place] and (description or discovery or early accounts)

--Boundaries
Focuses on the boundaries of places, whether established or in dispute (Library of Congress 2008a, H1333.5).

⊕ **BONUS FEATURE:** May include the text of related treaties.

--Territories and possessions
The definition: "those parts of a country that are subject to its government but not fully integrated into the nation to which they belong" (Library of Congress 2008a, H2185).
Consider also --**Colonies**.

--Foreign public opinion
Presents foreign opinion about a place or about topics relating to that place.
France--Foreign public opinion says that France is the place being judged. **France--Foreign public opinion, American** adds that it is Americans doing the judging.

America and the French nation, 1939-1945

We'll always have Paris: American tourists in France since 1930

POLITICS, CONFLICTS, AND DIPLOMACY

--Politics and government
For works that "discuss the theory, practice, and history of politics and government" (Library of Congress 2008a, H1942), this is the premier subdivision for works about running a country or other political entity.

--Kings and rulers
Describes works on the royals and royal houses of a country. For the running of that country, whether by monarchy or elected body, use **--Politics and government**.

--Political aspects
Addresses "the political dimensions or implications of nonpolitical topics" (Library of Congress 2008a, H1095). Fashion, the Internet, church attendance, our water supply—the variety confirms Aristotle's statement that "man is by nature a political animal."

--Political and social views
--Political activity
The Library of Congress separates the thinkers from the doers by providing these two subdivisions.

--Relations
"For general relations between one region or jurisdiction and another" (Library of Congress 2008a, H1996). Read "general relations" as anything goes. **Cuba and relations and United States** brings books on baseball and radio broadcasting, as well as more predictable topics like the Cold War.

ⓘ **NOTE:** If the number of places is three or more, the subdivision becomes **--Relations--Foreign countries**.

--Foreign relations
Specifically for formal diplomatic relations between sovereign states.

--Military relations
Not nearly as narrow as *military* makes it sound. These "non-hostile military relations and/or cooperation between one region or jurisdiction and another" (Library of Congress 2008a, H1996) are all over the map: hot spots and peace-keeping, covert and overt, prewar, postwar, cold war, what war?

> *The School of the Americas: Military training and political violence in the Americas*
>
> *Vendetta: Military medical peace operations in Kosovo*
>
> *More terrible than death: Massacres, drugs, and America's war in Colombia*
>
> *Russia's life-saver: Lend-lease aid to the U.S.S.R. in World War II*

--Boundaries
--Territorial questions
Boundary disputes are covered by **--Boundaries**, while **--Territorial questions** is for "territorial realignments, boundary questions, etc." resulting from wars (Library of Congress 2008a, H1333.5). A fine line there, so settle on this:

🔍 **MAGIC SEARCH:** [place] and (territorial questions or boundaries)

⊕ **BONUS FEATURE:** **--Boundaries** results sometimes include the texts of treaties.

--Campaigns
The student of the Battle of Waterloo will have plenty of catalog hits to choose from, given the scholarly output on the topic. But for minor or very recent skirmishes that have no separate book, **--Campaigns** wins the day. Also handy for overviews of the military actions in a particular conflict or region.

--Treaties
--Law and legislation
The Library of Congress (2008a, H2227) established precise boundaries for **--Treaties**, specifying that it be used only with "ethnic groups," "names of wars," and country names, and that within those confines it be used only for collections of treaties or books about treaties.

✅ **RULE:** Subject matter such as labor and copyright, which fall outside those three categories, receives the subdivision **--Law and legislation**. So it's **Choctaw Indians** (ethnic group) **and treaties** but **pollution and law and legislation**.

◉ **RECOMMENDATION:** The Library of Congress should allow catalogers to use **--Treaties** with any kind of subject matter, because the subdivision **--Law and legislation** is quite general and yields long lists of hits that may have nothing to do with treaties.

TOOLS FOR HISTORIANS

Historical research often demands a visit to specialized collections held by libraries, societies, and museums. The first set of "tools" subdivisions below helps the researcher plot the route, whether the trip be by interstate or Internet.

--Archives
--Sources
--Archival resources
--Library resources
--Manuscripts

These subdivisions are the power tools of the history trade, because they tell the researcher what documentary materials about a topic exist and, in most cases, where the materials reside. Search results are varied and remarkable:

> *British banking: A guide to historical records*
> *Theatre research resources in New York City*
> *A guide to Cherokee documents in foreign archives*
> *Hymnal collections of North America*

⊘ **RULE:** --**Archives** goes with people and organizations; --**Sources** goes with topics. In practice, searchers can leave such distinctions to catalogers and cast wide nets with these:

🔍 **MAGIC SEARCH:** [research interest] and (archiv* or sources or manuscripts)

🔍 **MAGIC SEARCH:** [research interest] and (library resources or archival resources or manuscripts)

--Historiography

Identifies a wide range of works that aid the historical researcher. Many study the trends in scholarship in a field and include judgments about the research that has been done. Others, such as *Computer applications to medieval studies,* present the practical side of research. *A guide to the history of California* does it all. In one chapter it describes the nature of the state's county records; in another it warns the reader of a list of books that present a history of prostitution in the state that is "marred by stereotypical images and exploitive interpretations" (Nunis and Lothrop 1989, 119).

--Societies, etc.
--Museums

Use these subdivisions to find out who cares about your area of research. The collections of large organizations rival those of libraries, and small organizations often house niche material that is not collected anywhere else.

--Genealogy
The Library of Congress (2008a, H1845) instructs catalogers to add this sub-division to "works of value in the study" of named families. Inside these works will be information from "family papers, deeds, wills, public records, parish registers, cemetery inscriptions, ship lists, etc."

⊕ **BONUS FEATURE:** --Genealogy is often attached to a place-name, the result being juicy tidbits of local history.

Consider also --Registers, which finds "lists of names of persons, organizations, or objects, etc., without addresses or other identifying data" (Library of Congress 2008a, H1095). Locate titles like *Index to Tennessee Confederate pension applications* or *Buncombe County, North Carolina apprenticeship bonds.*

--Chronology
These "what happened when?" works provide a valuable service to the researcher, and many are works of scholarship in their own right, going far beyond a simple list of dates.

--Census
"For works consisting of official counts of the population of a place or group, generally including vital statistics and other classified information relating to social and economic conditions" (Library of Congress 2008a, H1366).

--Early works to 1800
Historical in that the work described was originally published before 1800, and useful because catalog records list the publication date as the date of the reprinted edition, not the date of the original work.

⊕ **BONUS FEATURE:** Can be assigned only "as long as the original text has not been altered or reworked" (Library of Congress 2008a, H1576).

See also chapter 9, "Finding Primary Sources," chapter 5, "Finding Out about People: Individuals and Groups," chapter 8, "Finding True Stories: Memoirs, Observations, and Confessions," chapter 3, "Finding Images," chapter 11, "Tools for Scholars and Other Professionals."

CHAPTER 16

USEFUL FOR BUSINESS TOPICS

Most of these featured subdivisions pair up well with industries, business themes, or names of companies.

NOTE: Main headings for individual industries based on products have in the past been established under these various forms:

[Product] industries

[Product] industry

[Product] industries and trade

[Product] industry and trade

[Product] trade

Now, "in order to simplify and standardize headings for industries based on products, new industry headings are now being established using only the formulation [product heading] industry" (Library of Congress 2008a, H1673). Thank you, Library of Congress! This is a much-appreciated start, but more is needed.

⊚ **RECOMMENDATION:** Libraries should convert all the existing variations to the new standardized formulation, [Product] industry. Right now.

✪ **MAGIC SEARCH:** (industry or trade or industries) and [one of the following best all-around subdivisions] will cover a lot of territory.

BEST ALL-AROUND FOR BUSINESS

--[. . .] aspects
The prospect of finding an aspect to suit the situation is excellent. Take your pick from the following list:

--Economic aspects

--Environmental aspects

--Health aspects

--Moral and ethical aspects

--Political aspects

--Psychological aspects

--Religious aspects

--Social aspects

--Sociological aspects

--Case studies
Documents the "conditions of a particular field or activity" or can be used to examine an individual business (Library of Congress 2008a, H1350).

> *New ideas from dead CEOs: Lasting lessons from the corner office*
>
> *Productivity: Key to world competitiveness*
>
> *Enterprise wide strategic information systems planning for Shanghai Bell Corporation*

--Directories
Most libraries still have a choice selection of these incredible tomes in their collections. Indispensable for discovering details that you just cannot get anywhere else.

--Handbooks, manuals, etc.
From asset allocation to zero budgeting, handbooks will guide the way.

--Decision making

> *Investment blunders of the rich and famous—and what you can learn from them*
>
> *The triumph of contrarian investing: Crowds, manias, and beating the market by going against the grain*
>
> *Last chance to get it right: How to avoid the eight deadly mistakes made with money*

--Management
--Marketing
--Planning

DOING DAY-TO-DAY BUSINESS

--Accounting
--Auditing
--Customer service
--Finance
--Location
--Management--Decision making
--Records and correspondence

--Employees--Diseases

--Effect of technological innovations on

--Health and hygiene

--Job descriptions

--Legal status, laws, etc.

--Medical care

--Pensions

--Law and legislation

--Supply and demand

--Training of

--Personnel management
--Labor productivity

--Accidents
--Safety measures
Creating and maintaining a safe work environment with a Magic Search will keep the lawyers at bay. Disclaimer: The authors are not responsible for any legal action taken against your patrons!

MAGIC SEARCH (accidents or safety measures) and industr*

--Equipment and supplies
Very useful, but the Library of Congress (2008a, H1153) informs us that among all the industries the construction industry shall not have --**Equipment and supplies**. This unfortunate exclusion leaves backhoes, compressors, and the like out in the cold.

RECOMMENDATION: Library of Congress, please bring the construction industry in from the cold.

--Inventories
For listing things that are on hand at a particular time, such as year-end inventories, and any discussion of this activity. Surprisingly, this subdivision may not be used under retail trade or with individual businesses (Library of Congress 2008a, H1153).

⊘ **RECOMMENDATION:** Library of Congress, please do not exclude the retail trade and individual businesses.

--Energy conservation
--Energy consumption

--Materials management

THE PRODUCT

--Cost control
--Cost effectiveness

--Evaluation
Assesses products, services, equipment, activities, or an individual business.

--Inventory control
For industries and individual businesses, as opposed to the very limited use of **--Inventories**. This fine distinction borders on hairsplitting.

--Prices

--Production control
--Quality control
Discovers best processes used by industries to create the best product.

--Production standards
--Technological innovations
Discusses improvements that can increase efficiency and production.

--Trademarks

In this subsection several Magic Searches beckon to be employed: **[topic] and control, [topic] and costs, [topic] and energy, [topic] and production.**

OUTSIDE FORCES

--Cross-cultural studies
Appreciating how others around the world do business, and benefiting from this knowledge.

--Deregulation
--Economic conditions
--Economic conditions--Regional disparities

--Effect of [. . .] on
Businesses can suffer or benefit from myriad effects: terrorism, inflation, technological innovations, automation, wars, education, and let's not forget taxation.

--Forecasting
The next best thing to a crystal ball and probably about as reliable.

--Foreign ownership
Globalization hitting home—trends and issues.

--Law and legislation
--Safety regulations
--Standards

--Taxation
If it produces an income, then there will be taxes.

GETTING INTO TROUBLE OR KEEPING IT CLEAN

--Corrupt practices
Followed by the antidotes **--Moral and ethical aspects** and **--Professional ethics**.

--Cases
Finds compilations of court or regulatory agency decisions on legal topics concerning business.

--Trials, litigation, etc.
Combine with a company's name to find out about its day in court.

THE MARKET (INVESTMENTS, STOCKS, BONDS, DIVIDENDS, SECURITIES, SPECULATION)

--Charts, diagrams, etc.
Provides visual representations of numerical information on a topic, such as pie charts or bar graphs.

> *Technical analysis for the rest of us: What every investor needs to know to increase income, minimize risk, and achieve capital gains*

--Dictionaries
Know what business mavens are talking about and understand the concepts.

--Mathematical models
--Prices
--Prices--Statistics
--Ratings and rankings
--Tables

--Moral and ethical aspects

> *Stocking up on sin: How to crush the market with vice based investing*

or

> *Investing with your values: Making money and making a difference*

--Psychological aspects

> *Fear, greed and panic: The psychology of the stock market*

NOT-SO-SERIOUS BUSINESS

--Anecdotes
--Caricatures and cartoons
--Humor

> *The Dilbert principle: A cubicle's-eye view of bosses, meetings, management fads and other workplace afflictions*

⊗ **MAGIC SEARCH: [topic] and (anecdotes or cartoons or humor)**

CHAPTER 17

USEFUL FOR EDUCATION TOPICS

BEST ALL-AROUND

--Study and teaching
--Instruction and study
If you could have only one subdivision for education topics **--Study and teaching** would be it, because it serves both people wanting to learn a subject and people wanting to teach a subject. Use this terminology instead of the expected "teaching methods." Because the Library of Congress created a separate subdivision for music-related topics, **--Instruction and study**, the wannabe Renaissance crowd should consider this:

⭐ **MAGIC SEARCH:** [topic] and study

⊕ **BONUS FEATURE:** Teacher's editions, too!

--Education
--Knowledge and learning
--Training of
--In-service training
Precision rules here! **--Education** refers to works on education provided for groups of people (see chapter 5, "Finding Out about People"). **--Training of** is for methods of instructing occupational groups "to prepare them for employment" (Library of Congress 2008a, H2217). And **--Knowledge and learning** is used to describe the education, formal or informal, that an individual receives. In summary, Amish children get **--Education**, nurses get **--Training**, and George Bush gets **--Knowledge and learning**. (Nurses can get **--Education**, too, but if they're studying to be nurses, it's **--Training!**)

TEACHING AND LEARNING

--Problems, exercises, etc.

"Compilations of practice problems or exercises" (Library of Congress 2008a, H1095).

--Activity programs

A godsend to proponents of active learning, this describes "activities to be engaged in for the purpose of acquiring certain skills, concepts, or knowledge" (Library of Congress 2008a, H2110).

--Textbooks

In 2002, the Library of Congress dropped the restrictions on this subdivision and allowed it to be used to identify textbooks on any topic, not just religion and foreign languages, making it a workhorse for educators (Library of Congress 2008a, H2187). In the short time since 2002, **--Textbooks** already finds results for most areas of study, especially when used in a large catalog like the free-for-all OCLC WorldCat.org. **--Textbooks** also serves the education historian by uncovering resources about textbooks, such as *Lies my teacher told me: Everything your American history textbook got wrong.*

--Curricula

What to teach and plans for teaching it!

> *Take action! Lesson plans for the multicultural classroom*
> *The course syllabus: A learning-centered approach*
> *Ready, set, science! Putting research to work in K-8 science*

ASSESSMENT

--Evaluation

Educators who search with "assessment," will miss the boat. The Library of Congress uses **--Evaluation** to cover both the methods of assessing and the results themselves.

--Testing

--Ability testing for both "native aptitude" and "acquired proficiency" (Library of Congress 2008a, H2186).

--Intelligence testing
--Psychological testing
--Examinations

The overlap and inconsistency among these subdivisions test one's patience.

Note the two subject headings **Mathematical ability--Testing** and **Reading--Ability testing** and you will welcome this:

⊛**MAGIC SEARCH:** [topic] and (testing or examinations)

--Design and construction
For works on making examinations and tests (also bridges, gazebos, and zoos!).

> *Smart tests: Teacher-made tests that help students learn*
>
> *Systematic assessment of learning outcomes: Developing multiple-choice exams*

--Examinations, questions, etc.
"For compilations of questions and answers for examinations" about a topic (Library of Congress 2008a, H1095).

SCHOOLS

These straightforward subdivisions are used with educational institutions at all levels, from Miss Dana's Kindergarten Academy to Harvard U.

--Administration
--Finance
--Entrance examinations
--Entrance requirements
--Admission
--Buildings
--Sports
--Security measures
--Faculty
--Undergraduates and **--Graduate students** (Note the different forms! Why, Library of Congress, why?)
--Alumni and alumnae

CHAPTER 18

USEFUL FOR NATURAL AND PHYSICAL SCIENCES

Some areas in the sciences rely on more intricate subject analysis than other areas. The life sciences, chemicals, and materials are a case in point; these areas demand a different presentation.

Because the language of science can be highly specialized, this chapter includes definitions from *McGraw-Hill Dictionary of Scientific and Technical Terms,* written with the nonspecialist in mind. Other subdivisions need no further introduction and are just listed under special scientific concepts. Titles are added to give a fuller understanding of the subdivision when it seemed advantageous.

TOOLS OF THE TRADE

--Handbooks, manuals, etc.
"Arranged for ready reference and consultation" (Library of Congress 2008a, H1646).

> *Rapid guide to chemical incompatibilities*
>
> *A measure of everything: An illustrated guide to the science of measurement*
>
> *Springer handbook of atomic, molecular, and optical physics*
>
> *Beyond the solar system: 100 best deep sky objects for amateur astronomers*

--Methodology
Provides theory and practice combined.

> *Physics by inquiry: An introduction to physics and the physical sciences*

Sample preparation techniques in analytical chemistry

Kant's concept of geography and its relation to recent geographical thought

Biological investigations: Form, function, diversity and process

How science works: Evaluating evidence in biology and medicine

Selection methods in plant breeding

--Tables

Tables of physical and chemical constants and some mathematical functions

Correlation tables for the structural determination of organic compounds by ultraviolet light absorptiometry

Barlow's tables of squares, cubes, square roots, cube roots, and reciprocals of all integers up to 12,500

--Identification

Presents "the characteristics of a group for the purpose of determining the names of its members" (Library of Congress 2008a, H1095).

⊕ **BONUS FEATURE:** Identifies field guides for amateur naturalists and armchair forensic investigators. Elk tracks, oak leaves, bird songs, bones, rocks, and more.

--Technique

Describes "steps to be followed in performing a required task" (Library of Congress 2008a, H1095).

Analytical methods in forensic chemistry

Steroid analysis in the pharmaceutical industry

Cytological technique: The principles underlying routine methods

Solar observations: Techniques and interpretation

Environmental applications of geophysical surveying technique

--Laboratory manuals

"Workbooks containing concise background information and directions for performing work, including experiments, in the laboratory" (Library of Congress 2008a, H1095).

A demo a day: A year of physical science demonstrations

Lab math: A handbook of measurements, calculations, and other quantitative skills for use at the bench

A basic meteorology exercise manual

LIFE SCIENCES

Tools of the Trade for the Life Sciences

--Classification
--Nomenclature
"Systematic arrangement" of the scientific names of animals and plants (*McGraw-Hill dictionary of scientific and technical terms* [hereafter *McGraw-Hill dictionary*] 2003, 1431).

--Nomenclature, Popular
Systematic arrangement of the "common names" of animals and plants (Library of Congress 2008a, H1147).

🔍 **MAGIC SEARCH: [plant or animal] and (nomenclature or classification)**

Reproduction and Growth

--Reproduction
--Fertility
--Eggs
--Larvae
--Seeds
--Spores
--Fetus
--Embryology
--Nests
--Metamorphosis
--Life cycles
--Development
--Growth
--Mortality

Genetics

--Genetics
"The study of biological inheritance" (*McGraw-Hill dictionary* 2003, 893).

--Genetic engineering
"The intentional production of new genes and alterations of genomes by the substitution or addition of new genetic material" (*McGraw-Hill dictionary* 2003, 892).

--Breeding
"The application of genetic principles to the improvement of farm animals and cultivated plants" (*McGraw-Hill dictionary* 2003, 283).

--Hybridization
"Production of a hybrid by pairing complementary ribonucleic acid and deoxyribonucleic acid (DNA) strands" (*McGraw-Hill dictionary* 2003, 1022).

--Molecular genetics
"The approach which deals with the physics and chemistry of the processes of inheritance" (*McGraw-Hill dictionary* 2003, 1364).

Molecular and Cellular Biology
--Cytology
"Deals with the structure, behavior, growth, and reproduction of cells and the function and chemistry of cell components" (*McGraw-Hill dictionary* 2003, 540).

--Histology
"The study of the structure and chemical composition of animal and plant tissues as related to their function" (*McGraw-Hill dictionary* 2003, 998).

--Metabolism
"The physical and chemical processes by which foodstuffs are synthesized into complex elements[,] . . . complex substances are transformed into simple ones[,] . . . and energy is made available for use by an organism" (*McGraw-Hill dictionary* 2003, 1319).

Evolution and Ecology
--Origin
> *On the trail of the ancient opium poppy*
> *Origin and evolution of viruses*

--Evolution
--Adaptation

--Phylogeny
"The evolutionary or ancestral history of organisms" (*McGraw-Hill dictionary* 2003, 1590).

--Speciation
"The evolution of species" (*McGraw-Hill dictionary* 2003, 1988).

--Ecology
--Conservation

--Control

> *Killer bees: The Africanized honey bee in the Americas*
> *Kudzu, the vine to love or hate*

--Biological control

> *The bug book: Harmless insect controls*
> *Ecological management of agricultural weeds*
> *Silent spring*

--Climatic factors

Goes with plants, animals, and "land vehicles for works on the relation to those topics to climate" (Library of Congress 2007, SD-16).

> *The ferocious summer: Adélie penguins and the warming of Antarctica*
> *Study on car air conditioning system controlled by car occupants' skin temperatures*

--Effect of [. . .] on
   --Effect of acid precipitation on
   --Effect of dredging on
   --Effect of fires on
   --Effect of floods on
   --Effect of heavy metals on
   --Effect of turbidity on
   --Effect of ultraviolet radiation on
   --Effect of volcanic eruptions on

--Habitat

--Home range

"The area that an animal traverses in the scope of normal activities, such as feeding; not to be confused with territory" (Dunster and Dunster 1996, 164). **Consider also** --Territoriality.

--Reintroduction

> *When the wolves returned: Restoring nature's balance in Yellowstone*

--Migration

> *Hawk highway in the sky*
> *Underwater guideposts: Homing of salmon*

--Geographical distribution

> *Birds around the world: A geographical look at evolution and birds*
>
> *Distribution and systematics of the rabbits (Sylvilagus) of west-central Mexico*

Microbiology and Immunology, and More "-ologies"

--Microbiology

"The science and study of microorganisms, including protozoans, algae, fungi, bacteria, viruses, and rickettsiae" (*McGraw-Hill dictionary* 2003, 1333).

--Endocrinology

> *Bird hormones and bird migrations: Analyzing hormones in droppings and egg-yolks and assessing adaptations in long-distance migration*

--Immunology

"A branch of biological science concerned with the native or acquired resistance of higher animal forms and humans to infection with microorganisms" (*McGraw-Hill dictionary* 2003, 1054).

--Phenology

"The science which treats of periodic biological phenomena with relation to climate, especially seasonal changes" (*McGraw-Hill dictionary* 2003, 1576).

> *Phenology and growth habits of tropical trees: Long-term observations in the Bogor and Cibodas Botanic Gardens, Indonesia*

--Toxicology

> *Food contaminants and residue analysis*
>
> *Handbook of poisonous and injurious plants*

Also of Interest

--Physiology

Assigned to groups of people, individual and groups of animals and plants, and "individual organs and regions of the body" (Library of Congress 2006, 69).

--Morphology

"A branch of biology that deals with structure and form of an organism at any stage of its life history" (*McGraw-Hill dictionary* 2003, 1374).

--Anatomy
"A branch of morphology dealing with the structure of animals and plants" (*McGraw-Hill dictionary* 2003, 95).

--Nutrition
> *Food and health in early childhood*
> *Hunger and nutrition problems among American Indians*
> *Feeding your horse for life*

--Health
> *The sound hoof: Horse health from the ground up*
> *Your older cat: A complete guide to nutrition, natural health remedies, and veterinary care*

--Diseases
"An alteration of the dynamic interaction between an individual and his or her environment which is sufficient to be deleterious to the well-being of the individual and produce signs and symptoms" (*McGraw-Hill dictionary* 2003, 624).

--Behavior
> *Amphibians and their ways*
> *Social life of monkeys and apes*

--Psychology
"Mental processes and characteristics" of animals (Library of Congress 2008a, H1095).
> *Dolphin cognition and behavior*
> *Swarm intelligence: From natural to artificial systems*

--Sexual behavior
> *The evolution of courtship behavior in plethodontid salamanders*
> *Reproduction and fitness in baboons*

--Religious aspects
> *Animal sacrifices: Religious perspectives on the use of animals in science*
> *The spirit of trees: Science, symbiosis, and inspiration*

--Symbolic aspects

> *The language of flowers: Symbols and myths*
> *Irish trees: Myths, legends and folklore*

CHEMICALS

--Analysis
"The determination of the composition of a substance" (*McGraw-Hill dictionary* 2003, 93).

> *Analysis of complex hydrocarbon mixtures*

--Assaying
"For the determination of the quantity or quality of a metal in an ore, alloy, etc." (Library of Congress 2008a, H1149).

> *Determination of the precious metals*

--Carcinogenicity
Alerts that a substance might have the ability to produce cancer.

> *Benzene toxicity, carcinogenesis, and epidemiology*
> *Evaluation of carcinogenic potential of chemical mixtures containing arsenic and volatile organics*

--Diagnostic use
Describes a chemical's use in diagnosing diseases.

> *Copper and lymphomas*

--Environmental aspects

> *Lead, mercury, cadmium, and arsenic in the environment*
> *Why poison ourselves: A precautionary approach to synthetic chemical*

--Industrial applications
Science meets industry.

> *Organic building blocks of the chemical industry*
> *Chemical, biological, and industrial applications of infrared spectroscopy*

--Oxidation
"A chemical reaction that increases the oxygen content of a compound" (*McGraw-Hill dictionary* 2003, 1509).

--Physiological effect

> *The healing nutrients within: Facts, findings, and new research on amino acids*
>
> *Cadmium and health: A toxicological and epidemiological appraisal*

--Religious aspects

> *Fundamenta chymica; or, A sure guide into the high and rare mysteries of alchymie*
>
> *Chemistry, a gift from God*

--Spectra

Plural of spectrum, "the set of frequencies, wavelengths, or related quantities, involved in some process; for example, each element has a characteristic discrete spectrum for emission and absorption of light" (*McGraw-Hill dictionary* 2003, 1991).

> *Analysis of optically excited mercury molecules*
>
> *The atmospheric 60-GHz oxygen spectrum*

--Structure

> *Insulin: Chemistry, structure, and function of insulin and related hormones*

--Synthesis

"Any process or reaction for building up a complex compound by the union of simpler compounds or elements" (*McGraw-Hill dictionary* 2003, 2091).

> *The inorganic chemistry of materials: How to make things out of elements*

--Therapeutic use

Attached to topical headings (e.g., dreams, kudzu, estrogen).

> *Boronic acids: Preparation and applications in organic synthesis and medicine*
>
> *An element of hope: Radium and the response to cancer in Canada, 1900-1940*

⊘ **RULE:** If a book is about a drug, such as fluoxetine, the therapeutic nature is assumed and **--Therapeutic use** is "not valid under the heading Drugs and headings for individual drugs or groups of drugs" (Library of Congress 2008a, H1149). Catalogers are instructed instead to "use unsubdivided headings for individual drugs and groups of drugs for their therapeutic use" (H1149).

--Toxicology

Is arsenic an aphrodisiac? The sociochemistry of an element

Our children's toxic legacy: How science and law fail to protect us from pesticides

MATERIALS

The Library of Congress treats materials in two ways: by examining either the chemical aspects or the practical aspects. The practical examination holds few surprises. As always, some subdivisions just must be highlighted.

--Combustion

"The burning of gas liquid, or solid, in which the fuel is oxidized, evolving heat and often light" (*McGraw-Hill dictionary* 2003, 437).

Development of coal combustion sensitivity tests for smoke detectors

Wood energy guide for agricultural and small commercial applications

--Creep

"A time-dependent strain of solids caused by stress" (*McGraw-Hill dictionary* 2003, 506).

Creep and recovery

Fatigue and creep characteristics of materials for transportation and power industries

--Curing

Solar industrial process hot water as used to cure concrete blocks

--Defects

Yikes!

Cast iron defects analysis

Laser-induced damage of optical materials

--Density

Designing asphalt concrete for minimum optimum asphalt cement content

--Ductility

"The ability of a material to be plastically deformed by elongation, without fracture" (*McGraw-Hill dictionary* 2003, 661).

--Flammability

Fire-safe polymers and polymer composites

Combustibility of plastics

--Inclusions

Impurities in engineering materials

Metal fatigue: Effects of small defects and nonmetallic inclusions

--Recycling

*Iron and steel scrap: Its significance and influence on further
developments in the iron and steel industries*

How on earth do we recycle glass?

--Thermal properties

High temperature resistant polymers

Assessment of thermal embrittlement of cast stainless steels

--War use

The steel industry and the war effort

*Bronzes to bullets: Vichy and the destruction of French public statuary,
1941-1944*

CHAPTER 19

USEFUL FOR MEDICINE AND HEALTH TOPICS

GENERAL

--Encyclopedias
Provides a wide array of medical information, from a very broad look at a medical topic to an encyclopedic treatment of a single illness.

--Dictionaries
More than just words, many times with illustrations.

--Terminology
Knowing the correct terminology is a must for effective communication; this is especially true in the field of medicine.

--Handbooks, manuals, etc.
This workhorse will not let you down when searching for concise information on any medical topic.

--Health
--Health and hygiene
--Care and hygiene
Attached-to rules are coming out the ears! **--Health** goes with individuals; **--Health and hygiene** is attached to groups, ethnic, occupational, or otherwise; **--Care and hygiene** goes with parts of the body. Unless you have a particular individual in mind, use a Magic Search to find out about the health of people and their parts:

⭐ **MAGIC SEARCH: [group or body part] and hygiene**

--Popular works
Helps the layperson gain an understanding about a medical discipline, a specific disease, or diseases that befall a particular part of the body.

> *State of the heart: The practical guide to your heart and heart surgery*
> *American Cancer Society's complete guide to prostate cancer*
> *Plastic surgery: What you need to know—before, during, and after*

--Statistics
Provides numerical data about medical topics.

Ⓘ **NOTE:** The Library of Congress created two additional statistics subdivisions just for the world of medicine. **--Statistics, Medical** finds medical statistics about a place; **--Statistics, Vital** covers vital statistics for either a place or an ethnic group (Library of Congress 2008a, H2095). Health researchers will usually want to use this

🔍 **MAGIC SEARCH: [medical topic, place, or ethnic group] and statistics** to retrieve the widest range of titles.

> *Vision problems in the U.S.: Prevalence of adult vision impairment and age-related eye disease in America*
> *Observations on the increase and decrease of different diseases, and particularly of the plague*
> *Death stalks the Yakama: Epidemiological transitions and mortality on the Yakama Indian Reservation, 1888-1964*

⊕ **BONUS FEATURE:** You will have all the latest health numbers at your fingertips if your library catalog includes the free websites from national and international agencies, such as the U.S. National Library of Medicine, or the UN's World Health Organization.

BEST MEDICAL ILLUSTRATIONS EVER

--Atlases
Detailed illustrations galore!

HISTORICAL

--Chronology
Supplies a nice time line of important events, when things happened, and in what order.

--Early works to 1800
Affords a glimpse into the world of medicine in the very olden days.

> *A short discoverie of the unobserved dangers of severall sorts of ignorant and unconsiderate practisers of physicke in England* (from 1612)

> *A treatise wherein is declared the sufficiencie of English medicines, for cure of all diseases cured with medicine* (from 1580)

--History
Offers a look at the history of medicine, human diseases, medical ideas, medical technology, treatments, and much more.

PROFESSIONAL

--Case studies
"Professional description or analysis of one or more case histories on the topic" (Library of Congress 2008a, H1350). Excellent also for the just-curious crowd.

> *Street scenarios for the EMT and paramedic*

> *Chicken soup for the surviving soul: 101 stories of courage and inspiration from those who have survived cancer*

--Examinations, questions, etc.
--Outlines, syllabi, etc.
--Problems, exercises, etc.
Wonderful for preparing for a test or a quick review.

--Practice
Addresses professional practices in the medical field, including issues affecting the work environment.

> *Conceptual foundations: The bridge to professional nursing practice*

> *Inside pharmacy: The anatomy of a profession*

> *Symposium on issues for the practicing pediatrician*

--Professional ethics
--Moral and ethical aspects
The standards are high, and the temptations and pressures great!

> *The Hippocratic oath and the ethics of medicine*

> *Hooked: Ethics, the medical profession, and the pharmaceutical industry*

> *Oath betrayed: Torture, medical complicity, and the war on terror*

⊗ **MAGIC SEARCH:** [medical topic] and (moral or ethics)

CONDITIONS AND DISEASES

Medical conditions and diseases need special attention, even as far as subdivisions are concerned. Here is just a sampling:

--Abnormalities
Use with parts of the body.

--Age factors
This subdivision covers all the ages of man, but the search results cluster in the mature years.

> *The aging skeleton*
> *Geriatric ophthalmology*
> *Aging in muscle*

--Cancer
Use as a subdivision with parts of the body; **Cancer** is also a main heading.

--Diagnosis

--Diseases
Besides getting to diseases about parts of the body, this also fills us in about which diseases afflict groups of people, such as textile workers or athletes, and ethnic groups.

--Magnetic resonance imaging
Use for the more familiar MRI.

--Mortality
Who died? How many? Where did they die? What was the cause of death? If you combine --**Mortality** with a place, an ethnic group, or a medical condition, you will get the cold, hard facts.

⊕ **BONUS FEATURE:** There are lots of statistics here.

> *Disease and death in early colonial Mexico*
> *Capital crime: Black infant mortality in America*
> *Trends in cancer mortality in industrial countries*
> *Postservice mortality among Vietnam veterans*
> *Death in New England: Regional variations in mortality*

--Patients
Finds information about patients suffering with all types of medical conditions and ailments. Ranges from the very technical (*Differential fuel utilization and energy expenditure in patients with cystic fibrosis*) to personal stories useful for patient education (*Breathing for a living: A memoir*).

--Risk factors
--Prevention
Both wonderful by themselves; combining them alerts readers to the risks and provides information on therapies. **Diabetes and (risk factors or prevention)**, for instance.

--Tomography
This technical term is used instead of the more familiar *CT scan*.

--Wounds and injuries
Besides informing about wounds and injuries that afflict parts of the body, also covers wounds and injuries that happen to children, college athletes, and older people, for example, or to ethnic groups.

On the Mend Again

Many treatment and therapy options are available to treat what ails us. The options at our disposal include the following:

--Treatment and

> **--Alternative treatment**
> **--Chiropractic treatment**
> **--Dosimetric treatment**
> **--Homeopathic treatment**
> **--Palliative treatment**
> **--Diet therapy**
> **--Exercise therapy**
> **--Gene therapy**
> **--Hormone therapy**
> **--Physical therapy**

To get all the treatment options, use this:

⭐**MAGIC SEARCH: [ailment] and (treatment or therapy)**

ⓘ **NOTE:** This Magic Search will not capture **--Chemotherapy, --Radiotherapy,** and other subdivisions in which *therapy* is embedded.

--Rehabilitation

Gathers great resources for the clinician, and for patients and their caregivers.

> *Rehabilitation for traumatic brain injury*
>
> *Any day with hair is a good hair day: How to get through cancer and get on with your life*

For the clinician, the following Magic Search might pinpoint more relevant results:

⊛ **MAGIC SEARCH:** [ailment] and rehabilitation and not popular works

--Therapeutic use

Some things are supposed to be just plain good for us.

> *Antioxidants in nutrition, health, and disease*
>
> *Women and cannabis*
>
> *The cold water cure: Its principles, theory, and practice: with ample directions for its self-application and a full account of the wonderful cures performed with it on 7,000 patients of all nations*

CHAPTER 20

USEFUL FOR TECHNOLOGY TOPICS

--Handbooks, manuals, etc.
Great for consultation!

EC&M's electrical calculations handbook
The technology management handbook

--Periodicals
Look beyond the journals and magazines also described by **--Periodicals** and pick the annual publications with important updated information.

Square foot costs
Annual book of ASTM standards
The AED green book: Compilation of nationally averaged . . . rental rates and model specifications for construction equipment

--Case studies
Benefit from others' successes—or learn from their mistakes.

At home in the woods: Lessons learned in the wildland/urban interface
Invention by design: How engineers get from thought to thing
The technological fix: How people use technology to create and solve problems

--Standards

American national standard for safe use of optical fiber communication systems utilizing laser diode and LED sources

--Estimates
How much is all of this work going to cost?

> *Markup and profit: A contractor's guide*
> *Planning and estimating heavy construction*

--Mathematical models
Explaining it with numbers.

> *Mathematical modelling of chemical processes*

--Industrial applications
Industry meets the sciences.

> *Opto-mechatronic systems handbook: Techniques and applications*
> *Rapid prototyping: Laser-based and other technologies*

--Technological innovations

> *Fusion yields important benefits today*
> *Blown to bits: Your life, liberty, and happiness after the digital explosion*

--Design and construction
--Materials
--Measurements
--Specifications

--Effect of [. . .] on
A Magic Search of a topic and **effect** will bring many causes to light. There are many more causes and results waiting to be discovered.

⊛ **MAGIC SEARCH: [research interest] and effect**

> **--Effect of environment on**
> **--Effect of explosives on**
> **--Effect of lasers on**
> **--Effect of nearby construction on**
> **--Effect of temperature on**

--Testing
Will it fly?

> **--Compression testing**
> **--Dynamic testing**

--Environmental testing

--Fire testing

--Impact testing

--Nondestructive testing

--Sightings and encounters

For the less-than-factual side of technology.

Need to know: UFOs, the military, and intelligence

CHAPTER 21

THE BABY AND THE BATHWATER
Recommendations

All through this book readers have seen us recommend freewheeling keyword searches and say, "Ignore the rules." We meant it, but don't mistake our lightheartedness for not understanding the importance of good cataloging. Everything in this book is founded on one thing: catalogs built on the rock-solid Library of Congress subject heading system, including subdivisions. Without that foundation, no keyword search would hit the sweet spot and bring relevant results home.

At the highest level, library catalogs represent the "maintenance of the cultural record for future generations" (Yee 2007, 3). Librarians in the United States are very fortunate to be able to rely on the leadership and stewardship of Library of Congress for the creation of catalogs. In particular, the Library of Congress subject headings system (LCSH) is emerging as an international standard. In 2000, the National Library of Sweden created its Swedish Subject Headings, based on LCSH (Leth 2007) and on RAMEAU, the subject heading vocabulary used by the French national library, itself based on LCSH (Bibliothèque Nationale de France 2007). In 2007, the British Library announced the addition of 117,485 Library of Congress subject headings to the eighteenth-century records in the *English Short Title Catalogue*. And of course there's Google, which has decided to include library catalog records in its Google Book Search (OCLC 2008).

Here are our final recommendations, addressed to the many stakeholders.

REFERENCE LIBRARIANS

- Know your stuff—inside out!
- Know the structure of your catalog and of the databases you search.

- Add subdivisions to your lists of handy keywords. Incorporate them into your searching. Make a short list of the subdivisions that serve you best. Memorize it.
- Learn how subdivisions work. Read the introduction to *Library of Congress Subject Headings* to gain a better understanding of the subject heading system and to discover the invaluable pattern headings created for different disciplines.
- Advocate for full subject cataloging, performed by highly skilled catalogers. Let your administrators know that it is essential for providing excellent service to your community.
- Demand excellent subject access in expensive keyword-searchable databases.

CATALOGERS

We are counting on you to

- Read the *LCSH* rules carefully and assign subdivisions accurately.
- Be generous in assigning subject headings. Successful searches depend on the presence of multiple subject headings in a bibliographic record (Yee and Shatford Layne 1998).
- Use this book to help you understand what your colleagues in reference need.
- Counter arguments about cost-effectiveness with evidence of search-effectiveness.
- Take heart that your work is appreciated—and used.

LIBRARY ADMINISTRATORS

Please

- Be aware of the full effect of efficiency measures. Know that fine cataloging provides your library unique and lasting value, while poor cataloging is a lasting handicap. Martha Yee (2007, 5) expresses it well:

    Is it too much to ask for our colleagues in the profession, at least, to understand and acknowledge the value of human intervention for information organization, expensive though it is? Surely the richest country in the world can afford to pay for the human labor required to keep its cultural record in good order for future generations.

- Support your cataloging departments with informed personnel decisions that recognize the complexity of the work.
- Explain to other high-level decision makers the value of human intervention in the organization of information.

VENDORS AND PUBLISHERS

We call on you to

- Use this magnificent Library of Congress subject headings system in your products. The presence of subject headings—including subdivisions—is crucial in large full-text databases, where a keyword-in-full-text search yields long lists of irrelevant results.
- Invest in access points as well as in the digitization itself. Thousands of primary documents are wonderful, but we have to be able to find the one we need!

CATALOG AND DATABASE DESIGNERS

- Make subject headings prominent in results displays.
- Decouple with care! Terms connected to one another in subject headings offer the searcher an understanding of the relationships between concepts and topics. Yee and Shatford Layne (1998, 132) suggest, and we agree, that it is important to "keep the controlled vocabulary and the free text vocabulary distinct, so that the power of the controlled vocabulary is not lost."
- Retain meaningful labels on facet displays so the searcher can make informed choices.

INFORMATION AND LIBRARY SCIENCE EDUCATORS

- Teach, really teach, the organization of information.
- Present cataloging as the intellectual pursuit it is. Do not turn it into discussions of how to organize a supermarket (Yee 2007).
- Prepare your grads to know all the angles of professional searching—teach subject searching in reference classes in addition to strategies like Boolean logic.

LIBRARY OF CONGRESS

Thank you for the heartening *Response to On the Record: Report of the Library of Congress Working Group on the Future of Bibliographic Control* (Marcum 2008). In section 4 of the response document you reaffirm your commitment to the Library of Congress subject headings system. Many of your plans are ambitious, and we look forward to seeing the next steps.

These thoughtful changes are welcome, but let's agree to keep the baby when we change the bathwater. We've lived and breathed subdivisions for a good while now, and we see a few changes that would really improve the system.

- Choose between near-identical subdivisions: Currently, **--Instruction and study** is for music topics, but **--Study and teaching** is used for learning anything else!
- Replace perplexing definitions: A bibliography that is comprehensive and arranged by subject is assigned **--Indexes** rather than **--Bibliography**.
- Eliminate inconsistency. Why is it **--Graduate students**, but **--Undergraduates** instead of **--Undergraduate students**?
- Reduce! Do we really need **--Last years** and **--Last years and death** and **--Death** and **--Death and burial**?
- Go along with the crowd sometimes. Agree with the rest of the world that **--Biography** *is* about individuals! And that **--Education** *can* describe a person's schooling!

Once you have streamlined the subject heading system by correcting such confusing constructions, stick to your guns. Be proud of the system you created and work to keep it polished and powerful.

- Yes to **--Early works to 1800**!
- Yes to keeping **--Attitudes** and **--Public opinion** separate!
- Yes to any **--[. . .] aspects** you'll give us!

GENTLE READER

Follow our lead: subdivide and conquer!

ACKNOWLEDGMENTS

We wish to express our thanks to a number of people: our wonderful colleagues at Hunter Library, Western Carolina University, for their support; the many librarians whose enthusiasm for our original *Library Journal* article made us think this book would be worth writing; our dean of library services and our former university librarian, who believed in the project and proved it by lending us a well-equipped study room of our own; Chris Rhodes, our editor at ALA Editions, for his excellent guidance and impeccable timing; and our families, for their patience, encouragement, and love.

WORKS CITED

ALCTS Association for Library Collections and Technical Services. 2008. "Breaking down the silos: Planning for discovery tools for Library 2.0, an ALCTS symposium at ALA midwinter 2009." Retrieved from www.ala.org/ala/mgrps/divs/alcts/confevents/past/ala/mwinter/09/library2.0symp.cfm.

Bibliothèque Nationale de France. 2007. *Indexing policy: Historical background.* Retrieved from www.bnf.fr/PAGES/version_anglaise/cataloging/pol-ind_hist _eng.htm.

British Library. 2007. *Subject indexing. 117,485 Library of Congress Subject Headings (LCSH) added to 18th century records. 18th century records were not originally subject indexed.* Press release, September. Retrieved July 7, 2008, from www.bl.uk/collections/early/estcnews.html.

Chan, Lois. 2005. *Library of Congress subject headings: Principles and application.* 4th ed. Westport, CT: Libraries Unlimited.

Dunster, J., and K. Dunster. 1996. *Dictionary of natural resource management.* Vancouver: University of British Columbia Press.

Hobbs, J. B. 1999. *Homophones and homographs: An American dictionary.* 3rd ed. Jefferson, NC: McFarland.

Kornegay, Becky, Heidi Buchanan, and Hiddy Morgan. 2005. Amazing, magic searches! Subdivisions combine the precision of the cataloger with the free-wheeling style of a Googler. *Library Journal* 130, no. 18 (November): 44–46. Available from Academic Search Premier database.

Leth, P. 2007. *Subject Access—the Swedish Approach.* PowerPoint presentation at the EDL project workshop, Swedish National Library, November 23. Retrieved from the EDL Project website: www.edlproject.eu/workshop/down loads/Subject%20access%20-%20the%20Swedish%20approach.ppt.

Library of Congress. 2007. *Library of Congress subject headings.* 30th ed. Washington, DC: Library of Congress, Cataloging Distribution Service.

———. 2008a. Cataloger's Desktop. Retrieved October 2008, from http://desktop .loc.gov.

————. 2008b. *Library of Congress authorities.* May 19. Retrieved October 2008, from http://authorities.loc.gov.

Long, T. H., ed. 1979. *Longman dictionary of English idioms.* Harlow, England: Longman.

Mann, Thomas. 2005. *The Oxford Guide to Library Research.* 3rd ed. New York: Oxford University Press.

Marcum, D. B. 2008. Response to on the record: Report of the Library of Congress Working Group on the Future of Bibliographic Control. June. Retrieved from www.loc.gov/bibliographic-future/news/LCWGResponse-Marcum-Final -061008.pdf.

McGraw-Hill dictionary of scientific and technical terms. 6th ed. 2003. New York: McGraw-Hill.

Nunis, D. B., Jr., and G. R. Lothrop, eds. 1989. *A guide to the history of California.* New York: Greenwood.

OCLC. 2008. *OCLC and Google to exchange data, link digitized books to WorldCat.* Press release, May 19. Retrieved from www.oclc.org/news/ releases/200811.htm.

Publisher's Weekly. Web exclusive reviews: Week of 11/19. 2007. Retrieved from www.publishersweekly.com/article/CA6501885.html?q=%22young+stalin%22 +nondescript&.

Yee, M. M. 2007. Will the response of the library profession to the Internet be self-immolation? *The Unabashed Librarian,* no. 144 (August): 3–7.

Yee, M. M., and S. Shatford Layne. 1998. *Improving online public access catalogs.* Chicago: American Library Association.

INDEX

A

--Abbreviations, 16
--Abbreviations, acronyms, etc.,
   16
--Ability testing, 80
--Abnormalities, 112
--Accidents, 91
--Accounting, 91
--Acronyms, 16
--Activity programs, 96
--Adaptation, 101
--Administration, 97
--Admission, in schools, 97
--Adversaries
  biography, 32
  history, 83
--Aerial photographs, 11
--Aesthetics, 22, 28, 57
--Age factors
  conditions and diseases, 112
  social sciences, 74
--Alcohol use, 27
--Alumni and alumnae, 97
--Amateur's manuals, 4
--Analysis, in chemistry, 105
--Analysis, appreciation, in music,
   68
--Anatomy, 104
--Anecdotes
  business, 94
  places, 39
  true stories, 43
anthologies. See --Literary collections

--Antiquities
  groups, 34
  places, 38
--Apologetic works, 72
--Appreciation
  biography, 25
  humanities, 60
  uses of, 57
--Archival resources, 87
--Archives
  history, 83
  primary sources on people and
    organizations, 45
  tools for scholars, 87
  See also --Sources
art, 62–63
art, Asian, chronological subdivisions
   for, 50
--Art, vs. --Portraits, 10. See also --In art
--Art collections, 34, 63
[. . .] aspects
  business, 89–90
  uses of, 55–56
  See also magic searches for aspects of
   a topic
--Assassination, 84
--Assassination attempt, 84
--Assaying, in chemistry, 105
assessment in education, 96–97
--Atlases
  images of objects, 12
  medicine and health, 110
  scope, vi

--**Attitudes**
    of groups, 27
    scope, viii
    social sciences, 74
    uses of, 56–57
    See also --**Public opinion**
--**Attribution,** 63
--**Auditing,** 91
authors, biographies of, 24
--**Authorship,** 65–66

B

--**Behavior,** 104
--**Bibliography**
    and biography, 24
    humanities, 60
    readers' advisory, 67
    scholars, tools for, 52
    See also --**Indexes**
--**Bio-bibliography,** 59–60. *See also*
    --**Bibliography**
--**Biography**
    groups of people, 44
    life events, 23–24
    places, 36
    See also --**Personal narratives**
biography, in history, 83–84. *See also*
    true stories
--**Biological control,** 102
biology, 101, 103–105
--**Birth,** 22
--**Blogs,** 44
--**Bonsai collections,** 34
--**Book reviews,** 53. *See also* --**Reviews**
--**Books and reading**
    biography, 24
    readers' advisory, 67
botany. *See* science
--**Boundaries**
    history, 84, 86
    places, 39
--**Breeding,** 100
browsing of subject lists, viii
--**Buildings,** in schools, 97
--**Buildings, structures, etc.,** 37

business, 89–94
    humor, 94
    investments, 94
    legal aspects, 93
    management, 91–92
    outside forces on, 93
    products, 92

C

--**Campaigns,** 86
--**Cancer,** 112
--**Captivity**
    biography, 26
    history, 84
--**Carcinogenicity,** 105
--**Care and hygiene,** 109. *See also*
    --**Health and hygiene**
--**Caricatures and cartoons**
    business, 94
    images of people, 10
    primary sources, 47
    See also --**Parodies, imitations, etc.**
--**Case studies**
    business, 90
    medicine and health, 111
    social sciences, 73
    technology, 115
    true stories, 43
    See also --**Longitudinal studies**
--**Cases**
    business, 93
    law, 79
catalog and database designers,
    recommendations to, 120
catalogers, recommendations to, 119
--**Catalogs,** 12
--**Catalogs and collections,** 12, 34
--**Catalogues raisonnés,** 62
--**Cataphora,** vi
--**Catechisms,** 72
--**Census,** 88
--**Characters,** 66
--**Charts, diagrams, etc.**
    images, 9
    investments and stock market, 94

chemistry, 105–107
--**Chemotherapy,** 113
--**Childhood and youth,** 22–23
chronological subdivisions, 48–51
--**Chronology**
 history, 83
 humanities, 61
 medicine and health, 110
 time periods, 51
 tools for scholars, 53, 88
--**Citizen participation,** 76. *See also*
 --**Political activity**
--**Civilization**
 history, 82
 places, 38
 See also --**History**
"Classes of Persons" list, 22
--**Classification,** in life sciences, 100.
 See also --**Nomenclature**
--**Clergy,** 72
--**Climatic factors,** 102
--**Clothing,** 33
--**Coin collections,** 34
--**Collection and preservation,** 12
--**Collections,** 34
--**Collectors and collecting,** 12
--**Colonies,** 84
--**Combustion,** 107
--**Commerce,** 38
--**Comparative studies,** in religion, 71
--**Composition and exercises,** 64
--**Compression testing,** 116
--**Concordances**
 humanities, 60
 religion, 72
 See also --**Indexes**
--**Conduct of life,** 30
--**Conservation,** in ecology, 101
--**Conservation and restoration,** in art,
 63
--**Contemporaries**
 biography, 32–33
 history, 83
--**Contributions in,** 25
--**Control,** 102

--**Controversial literature,** in religion, 72
--**Conversation and phrase books**
 generally, 15
 language learning, 64
--**Conversion tables,** 20
--**Copying,** in art, 63
--**Correspondence**
 biography, 33
 primary sources, 45
 true stories, 44
 See also --**Records and**
 correspondence
--**Corrupt practices**
 business, 93
 law, 79
--**Cost control,** 92
--**Cost effectiveness,** 92
--**Court and courtiers,** 83
creative works, 40–42
--**Creeds,** 72
--**Creep,** 107
--**Criticism, Textual,** 59
--**Criticism and interpretation,** 59.
 See also --**History and Criticism**
--**Cross-cultural studies**
 business, 93
 social sciences, 74
CT scans. *See* --**Tomography**
--**Curing,** in materials science, 107
--**Curricula,** 96
--**Customer service,** 91
--**Customs and practices,** 71
--**Cytology,** 101

D

--**Death,** for groups, 23
--**Death and burial,** for individuals, 23
--**Death mask,** 34
--**Decision making,** 90
--**Defects,** 107
--**Density,** 107
--**Deregulation,** 93
--**Description and travel**
 historical places, 84
 images of places, 11

--**Description and travel** (cont.)
  places, 37
  travel, 8
  See also --**Conversation and phrase
    books**; --**Travel**, in biography
--**Design**
  art, 63
  do-it-yourself, 5
  images of objects, 12
--**Design and construction**
  art, 63
  do-it-yourself, 5
  education, 97
  images of objects, 12
  technology, 116
--**Designs and plans**
  art, 63
  do-it-yourself, 5
  images of objects, 12
--**Development,** 100
--**Diagnosis,** 112
--**Diagnostic use,** 105
--**Dialects,** 63–64
--**Diaries**
  biography, 29, 33
  primary sources, 45
  true stories, 44
dictionaries, 15–16
--**Dictionaries**
  descriptions of words, 14
  investments and stock market,
    94
  medicine and health, 109
  See also --**Glossaries, vocabularies,
    etc.**; --**Nomenclature;**
    --**Terminology;** --**Vocabulary**
--**Directories,** 90
--**Disciples,** 32
--**Discography,** 70
--**Discovery and exploration**
  history, 84
  places, 38
  rules, 11
discovery tools, ix
diseases, 112–114

--**Diseases**
  groups, 31
  life sciences, 104
  medicine and health, 112
--**Divorce,** 23
--**Doctrines,** 72
do-it-yourself guides, 5–6
--**Drama**
  creative treatments, 40
  performing arts, 70
--**Dramatic production,** 69
--**Drug use,** 27
drugs, 106
--**Ductility,** 107
--**Dwellings,** 33–34
--**Dynamic testing,** 116

E
--**Early accounts to 1600**
  history, 84
  places, 38
  rules, 11
  time periods, 51
--**Early works to . . . ,** 51
--**Early works to 1800**
  images of places, 11
  maps, 47
  medicine and health, 111
  places, 38
  tools for scholars, 88
ecology, 101–103
--**Ecology,** 101
--**Economic aspects**
  business, 90
  social sciences, 75–76
  uses of, 56
  See also --**Economic conditions**
--**Economic conditions**
  business, 93
  groups, 30
  history, 83
  places, 38
  social sciences, 75–76
  See also --**Economic aspects**

--Economic conditions--regional
  disparities, 93
education, 95–97
  assessment, 96–97
  schools, 97
  teaching and learning, 96
--Education
  education, 95
  for groups, 24
  See also --Knowledge and learning
--Effect of [. . .] on
  business, 93
  life sciences, 102
  technology, 116
  uses of, 57
--Eggs, 100
--Embryology, 100
--Emigration and immigration, 38
--Employees
  in business, 91
  as friends and associates, 32
--Employment, 25–26
--Encyclopedias
  general, 2
  medicine and health, 109
--Endocrinology, 103
--Energy conservation, 92
--Energy consumption, 92
--Entrance examinations, 97
--Entrance requirements, 97
--Environmental aspects
  business, 90
  chemistry, 105
  uses of, 56
--Environmental testing, 117
--Equipment and supplies, 91
--Errors of usage, 65
--Essence, genius, nature
  favorites, vi
  general, 2
  religion, 70
--Estimates, 116
--Ethics, 29, 57. *See also* --Moral and
  ethical aspects; --Professional
  ethics

ethnic groups. *See* groups of people
"Ethnic Groups" list, 22
--Ethnic relations, 38
--Ethnological collections, 34
--Ethnomusicological collections,
  34
etiquette, 30
--Etymology, 19, 64
etymology and word history, 19–20
--Euphemism, 18
--Evacuation and relocation, 84
--Evaluation
  education, 96
  products, 92
--Evolution, 101
evolution and ecology, 101–103
--Examinations, in education, 96.
  See also --Testing
--Examinations, questions, etc.
  education, 97
  how to review, 7
  medicine and health, 111
--Exhibitions, 12
--Exile, 84
--Expertising, 63

F
facet-based searching, ix
--Facsimiles
  humanities, 62
  maps, 47
  primary sources, 46
--Faculty, 97
--Family
  biography, 23, 31
  history, 83
--Family relationships, 32
FAQs, 3
--Fertility, 100
--Fetus, 100
--Fiction, 40
field guides. *See* --Identification
--Fieldwork, 54. *See also* --Laboratory
  manuals
--Filmography, 70

--Finance
  business, 91
  education, 97
--Fire testing, 117
--First performances, 70
--Flammability, 108
--Folklore, 66
--Forecasting
  business, 93
  time periods, 51
--Forecasts, 51
--Foreign countries, 77
--Foreign influences, 58
foreign languages
  --Conversation and phrase books, 15
  learning of, 7, 64
  --Vocabulary, 15
  See also language
--Foreign ownership, 93
--Foreign public opinion
  history, 85
  uses of, 57
  See also --Public opinion
--Foreign relations
  history, 85
  social sciences, 76
--Forgeries, 63
--Friends and associates
  biography, 32
  as dishy, vii
  history, 83

G

--Gazetteers, 16, 36
--Genealogy
  places, 38
  tools for scholars, 88
--Genetic engineering, 100
genetics, 100–101
--Genetics, 100. *See also* --Molecular
  genetics
--Geographical distribution, 103
--Geography, 39
geology, chronological subdivisions of,
  50

--Glossaries, vocabularies, etc., 15
Google Book Search, ix
--Government jargon, 18
--Graduate students, 97
--Grammar, 64
groups of people
  --Antiquities, 34
  --Attitudes, 27
  --Biography, 44
  --Death, 23
  --Diseases, 31
  --Economic conditions, 30
  --Education, 24
  "Ethnic Groups" list, 22
  --Family relationships, 32
  --Health and hygiene, 31
  --Humor, 30–31
  individuals vs. groups of people,
    22
  political activity of groups (*see*
    --Politics and government)
  --Politics and government, 26, 29
  --Relations with [group], 32
  --Religious life, 29
  --Social conditions, 30
  --Social life and customs, 30
  See also "Classes of Persons" list;
    magic searches for groups of
    people; people
--Growth, 100
--Guidebooks
  images of objects, 13
  images of places, 11
  places, 37
  travel, 8
  See also --Tours

H

--Habitat, 102
--Handbooks, manuals, etc.
  business, 90
  how-to guides, 4
  medicine and health, 109
  science, 98
  technology, 115

--Health
  biography, 31
  life sciences, 104
  medicine and health, 109
--Health and hygiene
  groups, 31
  medicine and health, 109
--Health aspects
  business, 90
  uses of, 56
--Herbarium, vi, 34
--Histology, 101
--Historical geography, 38
--Historiography, 52–53, 87
history, 82–88
  life and lives, 83–84
  medicine and health, 109–111
  places, 84–85
  politics, 85–86
  tools for scholars, 87–88
--History
  history, 82
  medicine and health, 111
  places, 38
--History and criticism
  humanities, 59
  music, 41
hobbies and --Guidebooks, 8
--Home range, 102
--Homes and haunts
  biography, 33–34
  humanities, 61
--Homonyms, 17
--Housing, 33
how-to guides, 4–8
  do-it-yourself, 5–6
  generally, 4–5
  languages, 7, 15, 64
  music, 6
  reviews, 7
  travel, 8
humanities, 59–72
  art, 62–63
  language, 63–65
  literature, 65–67

music, 68
  performing arts, 69–70
  readers' advisory, 67
--Humor
  business, 94
  groups and individuals, 30–31
  places, 39
--Hybridization, 101

I
--Identification
  images of objects, 13
  science, 99
--Idioms, 17
idioms and expressions, 17–18
--Illustrations, 13
images
  generally, 9–13
  medicine and health, 110
--Immunology, 103
--Impact testing, 117
--Imprisonment
  biography, 26
  history, 84
--In art
  art, 63
  creative works, 42
  images, 10
  vs. [. . .] in art, 10
  places, 39
--In bookplates, 39
--In literature
  creative works, 42
  places, 39
--In mass media, 39
--In motion pictures
  creative works, secondary, 42
  places, 39
--In popular culture, 39
--Inclusions, 108
--Indexes, 52–53. *See also*
       --Bibliography; --Concordances
individuals, life events of. *See* people
--Industrial applications
  chemistry, 105

--Industrial applications (cont.)
 technology, 116
industry, 89
--Inflection, 64
--Influence
 biography, 35
 humanities, 61
 uses of, 57
--[. . .] influences, 58
information and library science
 educator, recommendations to,
 120–121
initialisms, 16
--In-service training, 95. *See also*
 --Education
--Instruction and study
 education, 95
 music, 6, 68
--Intellectual life, 38
--Intelligence testing
 education, 96
 tests and measures, 80
 See also --Testing
--Interpretation (Phrasing, dynamics,
 etc.), 68
--Interviews
 primary sources, 46
 true stories, 43
 See also --Anecdotes
--Inventories, 92
--Inventory control, 92
investments, 94

J

--Jargon, 18
journals (diaries). *See* --Diaries
--Juvenile literature, 9

K

keyword-in-subject searches, viii, 82
--Kidnapping, 84
--Kings and rulers, 85. *See also*
 --Politics and government
--Knowledge--[topic], 24, 28

--Knowledge and learning
 biography, 24, 28
 education, 95

L

--Labor productivity, 91
--Laboratory manuals
 science, 99
 tools for scholars, 54
language, 7, 63–65. *See also* foreign
 languages
--Language--glossaries, etc., 18
--Larvae, 100
--Last years, 23
--Last years and death, 23
law, 78–80
--Law and legislation
 business, 93
 law, 78–79
 vs. --Treaties, 86
--Legal research, 79
--Legal status, laws, etc., 78–80
--Legends, 66
--Legislative history, vi
letters (correspondence). *See*
 --Correspondence
--Lexicography, 19–20
--Library, 34
library administrators,
 recommendations to, 119–120
library catalogs, searches available in, viii
Library of Congress, recommendations
 to, 121
Library of Congress Authorities
 chronological subdivisions, 50
Library of Congress Subject Headings, 119
--Library resources, 87
--Librettos, 70
--Life cycles, 100
life sciences, 100–105
 biology, 101, 103–105
 evolution and ecology, 101–103
 genetics, 100–101
 reproduction and growth, 100
--Literary art, 25

literary authors, biographies of, 24
--Literary collections
    creative treatments, 41
    places, 37–38
    readers' advisory, 67
literary genres, 40–42
--Literary style, 65–66
literature, 65–67. *See also* --In literature
--Liturgical objects, 72
--Liturgy, 72
--Location, 91
--Longitudinal studies
    social sciences, 73
    time periods, 51
    See also --Case studies

M

magic searches for aspects of a topic
    [research interest] and (influence or
      effect of), 58
    [topic] and aspects, 56
magic searches for chronological
    periods
    [topic] and (18* or 19th) and not
      18th, 50
magic searches for groups of people
    [activity/person/group] and (political
      activity or citizen participation), 76
    [group or body part] and hygiene, 109
    [group or topic] and testing, 80
    [individual or group] and (pictorial
      works or portraits), 10
    [medical topic, place, or ethnic
      group] and statistics, 110
    [person or group] and (health or
      diseases), 31
    [person or group] and (mental health
      or psychology), 75
    [person or group of people] and
      (imprisonment or captivity), 84
    [research interest or person/group]
      and quotations, 19
magic searches for how-to guides
    [topic] and (examinations or
      problems or study guides), 7

    [topic of interest] and (manuals or
      technique), 5
    [your how-to interest] and repair*, 6
    [your interest] and design*, 5
    [your musical interest] and
      (instruction or self-instruction), 6
magic searches for images
    [individual or group] and (pictorial
      works or portraits), 10
    [object] and (design*), 12
    [place] and (pictorial works
      or guidebooks or tours or
      description), 11
    [place-name] and (early works or
      early accounts or discovery), 11
    [research interest] and (collect* or
      catalogs or exhibitions), 12
magic searches for people
    [activity/person/group] and
      (political activity or citizen
      participation), 76
    [group or topic] and testing, 80
    [individual or group] and (pictorial
      works or portraits), 10
    [person] and (appreciation or
      influence), 61
    [person] and knowledge, 28
    [person or group] and (health or
      diseases), 31
    [person or group] and (mental health
      or psychology), 75
    [person or group of people] and
      (imprisonment or captivity), 84
    [person's name] and (associates or
      adversaries or contemporaries or
      relations with), 33
    [person's name] and collections, 34
    [person's name] and (death or last
      years), 23
    [play or playwright] and (dramatic
      production or stage history), 69
    [research interest or person] and
      (anecdotes or interviews or case
      studies or personal narratives or
      biography), 44

magic searches for people (cont.)
[research interest or person] and
(correspondence or diaries or
personal narratives or blogs), 44
[your author or genre] and (technique
or style or authorship), 66
See also magic searches for groups
of people
magic searches for places
[place] and (description or discovery
or early accounts), 84
[place] and (description or
guidebooks or tours), 37
[place] and (pictorial works
or guidebooks or tours or
description), 11
[place] and (territorial questions
or boundaries), 86
[place-name] and (early works or
early accounts or discovery), 11
[places] and relations, 77
magic searches for primary sources
[research interest] and (archives
or sources or diaries or
correspondence or narratives
or interviews or facsimiles), 46
[research interest] and
correspondence, 45
[research interest] and (interviews
or personal narratives), 46
[research interest] and (sources or
archives), 45
magic searches for scholarly topics
[research interest] and reviews, 54
[topic] and (bibliography or indexes
or historiography), 53
[topic] and (methodology or
research), 54
magic searches for true stories
[research interest or person] and
(anecdotes or interviews or case
studies or personal narratives or
biography), 44
[research interest or person] and
(correspondence or diaries or
personal narratives or blogs), 44

magic searches for words
[area of interest] and (abbreviations
or acronyms), 16
[language] and (glossaries or
vocabulary or phrase), 15
[research interest or person/group]
and quotations, 19
magic searches in business
(accidents or safety measures) and
industr*, 91
(industry or trade or industries)
and [one of the best all-around
subdivisions], 89
[topic] and (anecdotes or cartoons
or humor), 94
[topic] and control, 92
[topic] and costs, 92
[topic] and energy, 92
[topic] and production, 92
magic searches in education
[topic] and study, 95
[topic] and (testing or examinations), 97
magic searches in history
[person or group of people] and
(imprisonment or captivity), 84
[place] and (description or discovery
or early accounts), 84
[place] and (territorial questions
or boundaries), 86
[research interest] and (archiv*
or sources or manuscripts), 87
[research interest] and (library
resources or archival resources
or manuscripts), 87
magic searches in humanities
[instrument] and (methods or
exercises or instruction), 68
[object] and design, 63
[person] and (appreciation or
influence), 61
[play or playwright] and (dramatic
production or stage history), 69
[research interest] and (legends or
folklore), 67
[research interest] and (religious
aspects or religious life), 71

[your author or genre] and (technique or style or authorship), 66
magic searches in medicine and health
[ailment] and rehabilitation and not popular works, 114
[ailment] and (treatment or therapy), 113
[group or body part] and hygiene, 109
[medical topic] and (moral or ethics), 112
[medical topic, place, or ethnic group] and statistics, 110
magic searches in science
[plant or animal] and (nomenclature or classification), 100
magic searches in social sciences
[activity/person/group] and (political activity or citizen participation), 76
[group or topic] and testing, 80
[person or group] and (mental health or psychology), 75
[places] and relations, 77
[research interest] and (economic conditions or economic aspects), 75
[research interest] and (social or sociological) and (aspects or conditions), 78
magic searches in technology
[research interest] and effect, 116
--Magnetic resonance imaging, 112
--Maintenance and repair, 5
--Management, 90
--Management--Decision making, 91
manuals. *See* --Handbooks, manuals, etc.
manuscripts, original, 62
--Manuscripts, works about manuscripts
humanities, 62
tools for scholars, 87
See also --Archives; --Early works to 1800; --Notebooks, sketchbooks, etc.
--Map collections, 34
--Maps
places, 39
primary sources, 47
--Marketing, 90
--Marriage, 23

--Materials, 116
--Materials management, 92
materials science, 107–108
--Mathematical models
investments and stock market, 94
technology, 116
--Mathematics, 20
--Measurements, 116
medicine and health, 109–114
diseases, 112–114
history, 109–111
professional concerns, 111–112
memoirs, 43–44
--Mental health
biography, 31
social sciences, 75
--Mental health services, 75
--Metabolism, 101
--Metamorphosis, 100
--Methodology
science, 98–99
tests and measures, 80–81
tools for scholars, 54
--Methods, in music, 68
--Microbiology, 103
--Migration, 102
--Military relations, 86
--Miscellanea, vii, 3
--Missions, 72
--Mistresses, vii
--Molecular genetics, 101
--Monuments, 34
--Mood, in languages, vii
--Moral and ethical aspects
business, 90, 93, 94
law, 80
medicine and health, 111
uses of, 56
See also --Ethics
--Moral conditions, 38
morals, 30
--Morphology, 103
--Mortality
life sciences, 100
medicine and health, 112
motifs. *See* --Themes, motives

motion pictures. *See* **--In motion pictures**
movies. *See* **--Drama**
--Museums, 87
music, 49, 68
--Musical instrument collections, 34
--Musical settings
creative treatments, 42
music, 68
--Mythology, 67

N

--Names, vi
"Names of Persons" list, 22
natural history. *See* science
--Natural history collections, 34
--Nests, 100
--New words, 19
--Nomenclature, 15
life sciences, 100
--Nomenclature, Popular, 100
--Nondestructive testing, 117
--Notebooks, sketchbooks, etc.
biography, 29
favorites, vi
humanities, 61–62
primary sources, 47
novels, 40
numbers, 20–21
--Numismatic collections, 34
--Nutrition, 104

O

--Obituaries, 35
objects, images of, 11–13
--Obscene words, 18
--Observations, 21
--Obsolete words, 19
--On postage stamps, 39
--On television, 39
--Origin, 101
--Outlines, syllabi, etc.
general, 1
medicine and health, 111
--Oxidation, 105

P

--Pamphlets, 46
--Paramours, vii, 83
--Parodies, imitations, etc., 41. *See also* **--Caricatures and cartoons; --Humor**
--Patients, 113
people, 22–35
activities of, 24–27
--Archives, 45
conditions of, 30–31
family and associates, 31–33
individuals vs. groups of people, 22
--Language--Glossaries, etc., 18
life events of, 22–24
--Musical settings, 42
--Portraits, 10, 47
possessions of, 33–34
true stories and memoirs, 43–44
views and thoughts of, 27–30
See also groups of people; magic searches for people
--Performances
biography, 25
performing arts, 69
See also **--First performances**
performing arts, 60, 69–70
--Periodicals
technology, 115
tools for scholars, 53
--Personal narratives
primary sources, 45–46
true stories, 44
See also **--Biography**
--Personnel management, 91
--Phenology, 103
--Philosophy, in biography, 27
--Phonology, 64
--Photograph collections, 34
--Photographs
primary sources, 47
rules, 13
--Photographs from space, 11
--Phylogeny, 101
--Physiological aspects, 56

--**Physiological effect,** 106
--**Physiology,** 103
--**Pictorial works**
  creative treatments, 42
  images, 9
  images of objects, 11
  images of people, 10
  images of places, 10
  places, 38
  primary sources, 47
  scope, 9, 38
place names, 16, 36
places, 36–39
  gazetteers, 16, 36
  history, 84–85
  images of, 10–11
  --**Quotations, maxims, etc.,** 18–19
  time periods, 48–49
  See also magic searches for
    places
--**Planning,** 90
plural and singular, distinctions
  between, viii
--**Poetry,** 41
--**Political activity**
  biography, 26
  history, 85
  social sciences, 76
--**Political and social views**
  biography, 29
  history, 85
  social sciences, 76
  use of, 57
--**Political aspects**
  business, 90
  history, 85
  social sciences, 76
  uses of, 56
political science, 75–77
--**Politics and government**
  activities of ethnic groups, 26, 29
  government jargon, 18
  history, 85
  places, 38
  social sciences, 75
politics and history, 85–86

--**Popular works**
  general, 2
  images, 9
  medicine and health, 110
--**Portraits**
  images of people, 10
  primary sources, 47
--**Practice,** 111
--**Prayers and devotions,** 71, 72
--**Pre-existence,** 22
--**Prevention,** of diseases, 113
--**Prices,** 92, 94
--**Prices--Statistics,** 94
primary sources, 45–47
--**Private collections,** 34
pro and con arguments. *See* --**Public
  opinion**
--**Problems, exercises, etc.**
  general, 2
  how to review, 7
  medicine and health, 111
  teaching and learning, 96
--**Production and direction,** 69
--**Production control,** 92
--**Production standards,** 92
profanity, 18
--**Professional ethics**
  business, 93
  medicine and health, 111
  See also --**Ethics**
--**Pronunciation,** 65
--**Pronunciation by foreign speakers,** 70
--**Prophecies,** 72
--**Psychological aspects**
  business, 90, 94
  social sciences, 73–74
  uses of, 55
--**Psychological testing**
  education, 96
  tests and measures, 80
  See also --**Testing**
psychology, 75
--**Psychology**
  biography, 30
  life sciences, 104
  social sciences, 74

--Public opinion
  social sciences, 74
  uses of, 57
  See also --Attitudes; --Foreign public opinion
publishers, recommendations to, 120

Q

Q&A formatted works, 3
--Quality control, 92
quotations, 18–19
--Quotations
  biography, 29–30
  generally, 18
--Quotations, maxims, etc., 18–19

R

--Race relations, 38
--Radiotherapy, 113
--Ratings and rankings, 94
readers' advisory, 67
recommendations, 118–121
--Records and correspondence
  business, 91
  sources, 45
  See also --Correspondence
--Recreation, 26
--Recycling, 108
reference librarians, recommendations to, 118–119
--Registers, 88
--Rehabilitation, 114
--Reintroduction, 102
--Relations
  history, 85
  politics, conflicts, and diplomacy, 85
  social sciences, 76–77
  See also --Ethnic relations; --Military relations; --Race relations
--Relations with [group], 32
--Relations with men, 32
--Relations with women, 32
religion, 70–72
--Religion
  biography, 29

generally, 70
places, 38
views on, 57
--Religious aspects
  business, 90
  chemistry, 106
  humanities, 71
  life sciences, 104
--Religious life
  of groups, 29
  humanities, 71
--Religious life and customs
  humanities, 71
  places, 38
--Repairing, 6
--Reproduction, in art, 63
--Reproduction, in life sciences, 100
reproduction and growth, 100
--Research, 54. *See also* --Methodology
--Reverse indexes, 16–17
--Reviews
  performing arts, 70
  tools for scholars, 53–54
reviews for tests. *See* --Examinations, questions, etc.; --Outlines, syllabi, etc.; --Problems, exercises, etc.
--Risk factors, 113
--Rituals, 72
--Romances, 67
Rule of A.D. 1400, 10

S

--Safety measures, 91
--Safety regulations, 93
scholarly tools, 52–54
--Schooling, vii
schools, 97
science, 98–108
  chemistry, 105–107
  life sciences, 100–105
  materials science, 107–108
--Scientific apparatus collections, 34
--Scores, 68
searches, types of, viii
--Security measures, 97

--Seeds, 100
self-help books. *See* **--Conduct of life;**
   --Psychological aspects
--Self-instruction
   languages, 7
   music, 6
sense of humor. *See* **--Humor**
--Sermons, 72
--Sex differences, 74
--Sexual behavior
   biography, 27
   life sciences, 104
short stories, 40
--Shrines, 34
--Sightings and encounters, 117
singular and plural, distinctions
      between, viii
--Slang, 18
--Social aspects
   business, 90
   social sciences, 77–78
   uses of, 55
--Social conditions
   groups, 30
   history, 83
   places, 38
   social sciences, 77–78
--Social life and customs
   groups, 30
   history, 83
   places, 36
   scope, vii
   social sciences, 73
   travel, 8
social sciences, 73–81
   law, 78–80
   political science, 75–77
   psychology, 75
   sociology, 77–78
   tests and measures, 80–81
--Societies, etc., 87
--Sociological aspects
   business, 90
   social sciences, 77–78
sociology, 77–78

--Songs and music
   biography, 34
   creative treatments, 41
   music, 68
   places, 39
--Sources
   biography, 28
   history, 83
   rules, 45
   tools for scholars, 87
   uses of, 58
sources, primary, 45–47
--Speciation, 101
--Specifications
   images of objects, 13
   technology, 116
--Spectra, 106
--Spores, 100
--Sports, 97
--Spurious and doubtful works, 27
--Stage history, 69
--Stage-setting and scenery, 69
--Stamp collections, 34
--Standards
   business, 93
   technology, 115
   tools for scholars, 54
--Statistical methods
   numbers, 20–21
   tests and measures, 81
   tools for scholars, 54
--Statistical services, 81
statistics. *See* **--Mortality**
--Statistics
   generally, 20
   medicine and health, 110
   places, 39
   tests and measures, 81
--Statistics, Medical, 110
--Statistics, Vital, 110
--Statues, 34
--Stories, plots, etc.
   humanities, 60
   readers' advisory, 67
   See also **--Themes, motives**

--Structure, 106
--Studies and exercises, in music, 68
--Study and teaching
    education, 95
    teach yourself anything, 6
    See also --Instruction and study
--Study guides, 7
--Style, 65
--Style manuals, 65
Subject Cataloging Manual, vii–viii
--Substance use, 27
--Symbolic aspects, 105
--Synonyms and antonyms, 16
--Synthesis, 106

T

--Tables
    investments and stock market, 94
    mathematics, 20
    science, 99
--Taxation, 93
teaching and learning, 96
--Teaching pieces, in music, 68
--Technique
    how-to guides, 4
    literature, 65–66
    science, 99
--Technological innovations
    products, 92
    technology, 116
technology, 115–117
television shows. *See* --Drama
--Terminology, vi
    medicine and health, 109
    not quite dictionaries, 14
    tools for scholars, 53
--Terms and phrases, vs. dictionary-type
    subdivisions, vi, 17
--Territorial questions, 86. *See also*
    --Boundaries
--Territoriality, 102
--Territories and possessions, 84
--Testing
    education, 96

technology, 116–117
tests and measures, 80
tests and measures, 80–81
--Textbooks
    general, 1
    limits in application of, before 2002, 2
    scope before 2002, 6
    teach yourself anything, 6
    teaching and learning, 96
--Textbooks for foreign speakers, 7, 64
--Themes, motives
    humanities, 61
    readers' advisory, 67
    See also --Stories, plots, etc.
--Theology, 72
--Therapeutic use
    chemistry, 106
    medicine, 114
--Therapy, 113
--Thermal properties, 108
thesauri, 16
time periods, 48–51
    digits in, 49
    examples, 48–50
--Tobacco use, 27
--Tomb/tombs, 34
--Tomography, 113
tools for scholars
    generally, 52–54
    history, 87–88
--Tours
    images of places, 11
    places, 37
    travel, 8
    See also --Guidebooks
--Toxicology
    chemistry, 107
    life sciences, 103
trade, 89
--Trademarks, 92
--Training of, in education, 95. *See also*
    --Education
--Travel, in biography, 27. *See also*
    --Description and travel
--Treaties, 86. *See also* --Boundaries

--Treatment, 113
--Trials, litigation, etc.
  biography, 26
  business, 93
  law, 79
true stories, 43–44

U
--Undergraduates, 97
--Usage, 65

V
vendors and publishers,
    recommendations to, 120
--Versions, 72
--Views on, 28, 56–57. *See also*
    --Attitudes; --Political and social
    views
--Vocabulary, 15
--Vocational guidance, 5

W
--War use, 108
word usage, 16–17
words, 14–20
WorldCat, viii–ix
--Wounds and injuries, 113

Z
zoology. *See* science

You may also be interested in

Virtual Reference Best Practices: When it comes to virtual reference, one size doesn't fit all. What works in one library won't necessarily work in another. How do you figure out what to do? The recently published Virtual Reference Service Guidelines from the Reference and User Services Association (RUSA) provide the starting point. Kern, a leading virtual reference expert, outlines the tools and decision-making processes that will help you and your library evaluate, tailor, and launch virtual reference services that are a perfect fit for your community and your library.

Sequels, 4th ed.: The most popular and long-lasting guide to novels in series returns with greatly expanded series listings. Mysteries continue to be a mainstay, with fantasy, science fiction, and romance listings, plus non–genre fiction selections from authors such as Edward Abbey and Lawrence Durrell. The authors have carefully sifted through a growing group of series to select those most likely to be available in a medium-sized public library, weeding out esoteric, obscure, and less-popular series. This classic reference includes hundreds of annotated series, a title index, and suggestions for reading order.

Reference Sources for Small and Medium-Sized Libraries,

7th ed.: This book includes the best of the best and most affordable resources, websites, CD-ROMS, and electronic databases, as well as print. The editors provide an introductory overview of the topics, then list their recommended selections with insightful annotations on each source. Specifications for each source (author/editor, publisher, format, price range, and Dewey and Library of Congress call numbers) make it easy to access the resources. Library patrons will find this an invaluable resource for current everyday topics, and librarians will appreciate it as a reference and collection development tool.

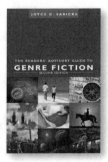

The Readers' Advisory Guide to Genre Fiction, 2nd ed.: This revised edition provides a way of understanding the vast universe of genre fiction in an easy-to-use format. Expert readers' advisor Joyce Saricks offers groundbreaking reconsideration of the connections between genres, providing key authors and themes within fifteen genres, an explanation of how the different genres overlap, the elements of fiction most likely to entice readers, and much more.

Check out these and other great titles at www.alastore.ala.org!